A GUIDE TO THE BEACHES AND BATTLEFIELDS OF
NORMANDY

A GUIDE TO THE BEACHES AND BATTLEFIELDS OF
NORMANDY

DAVID EVANS

AMBERLEY

To Frank Horrocks and many others like him who took part in the events in Normandy during 1944 but have never been back ... yet.

First published 1995 by Michael Joseph

This edition published 2010

Amberley Publishing
Cirencester Road, Chalford,
Stroud, Gloucestershire, GL6 8PE

www.amberley-books.com

British Library Cataloguing in Publication Data.
A catalogue record for this book is available from the British Library.

ISBN 978 1 84868 184 2

Typesetting and origination by Amberley Publishing
Printed in Great Britain

CONTENTS

ILLUSTRATIONS

MAPS

(Copyright holders are indicated in italics.)

FOREWORD

I feel most privileged to be invited to write a few words about this fascinating book which David Evans has written following long and detailed research whilst, for the purpose of it, he and his wife lived for much of over two years in Normandy.

When the monumentous events he has written about were taking place he was a pupil at Llandovery College in West Wales. I feel sure that, as they unfolded, the reports of them absorbed the inquiring mind of the literary figure and careful and scrupulous historian that David Evans has certainly become.

He calls his book a Guide. So, in part, it is, and as such it will prove lastingly invaluable to all who go to Normandy to see and to explore the battlegrounds of the Second World War and to try to comprehend how so many men, along with their arms and supplies, fought one another in such close countryside in a relatively small part of France. It was then a very crowded, tempestuous place.

But for those of us who fought in Normandy and who survive to read this book it rolls back our memories for almost half a century. There we are again among the little orchards alongside our comrades and at times almost touching the foe amidst the noise, the dust, the carnage, the penetrating and repulsive smells, the thunder of big guns, the thump of mortars and, what is the deepest impression of all on the mind, the sacrifice of life made every minute of every day.

This book expertly guides the visitor to Normandy, and will be a companion to living ex-servicemen who served there. It is also an eloquent tribute to those who died in the freshness of youth.

The Rt. Hon. Sir Tasker Watkins
VC, GBE, PC, DL

PREFACE

'Soldiers, Sailors and Airmen
of the Allied Expeditionary Force!
You are about to embark upon a Great Crusade ...'

General Dwight D. Eisenhower, Supreme Allied Commander,
June 1944

For the most famous events in our history, the year is usually sufficient – 1066, 1485, 1666, 1815. Few dates are remembered by the day, month and year, but there are some – 1 July 1916, the first day of the Battle of the Somme, and 6 June 1944, D-Day.

In the dark days of 1940, Winston Churchill had promised, *'Britain will fight on ... if necessary for years ... We shall go back.'* On the morning of 6 June 1944 his promise was kept.

Fifty years later, the epic story of D-Day has lost none of its appeal. Each year, veterans, relatives, tourists and school parties return to the beaches and battlefields of Normandy. For many, it is out of interest – a chance to visit places they have read about or seen in the film *The Longest Day* – but for some it is a pilgrimage.

This book first describes the background to Operation *Overlord* and then outlines the events of D-Day and the opening stages in the battle for Caen. Contemporary newspaper reports and cartoons help to create something of the atmosphere of the time. The remainder of the book is not a guide in the usual sense. It recommends no tours, since a pre-planned series of visits to battle sites and monuments can often prove tedious. Instead, it provides maps and gives all the essential information – the location of each town, village, beach, battery and cemetery, gives some idea of what happened there on D-Day and describes what remains to be seen today. It allows visitors to plan their own itineraries and so provide for their own particular needs and interests.

For help in the preparation of this book I am much indebted to the following: the Air Historical Branch (RAF) and Naval Historical Section (Ministry of Defence), the National Archives of Canada, the National Archives of the United States (Washington), the Imperial War Museum, the Public Record Office, the Commonwealth War Graves Commission, the

Hampshire Library Service (Eastleigh and Eastern Branch, Southampton), the *Memorial-Un Museé Pour la Paix* (Caen), *Museé Memorial de la Bataille de Normandie* (Bayeux), the regimental headquarters and museums of The Airborne Forces, The Devonshire and Dorset Regiments, The Duke of Cornwall's Light Infantry, The Durham Light Infantry, The Queen's Own Highlanders, The Royal Army Chaplains' Department, The Royal Green Jackets, The Royal Hampshire Regiment, The Royal Military Police, The Royal Regiment of Fusiliers, The Royal Regiment of Wales, The Royal Signals, The Staffordshire Regiment, and The Worcestershire and Sherwood Foresters Regiment, the late Wing Commander Frederick Carroll, Louis Lecanu, Guy and Nelly Herry, Roland Flauhaut, Vic Cooper and Dr Claude Bamber. I am also most grateful to Mme. Morel for her unfailing hospitality during my frequent visits to the Hotel de Brunville in Bayeux.

Finally, my gratitude to my wife, Carol, for hours of patient note taking, and for navigating the roads of Normandy. Without her encouragement and support this book would not have been started let alone finished.

David Evans

1

BACKGROUND – THE EUROPEAN WAR

At dawn on the morning of 1 September 1939, German forces invaded Poland and for the second time in a quarter of a century Europe was plunged into war. With Britain and France on one side and Germany on the other, it was a near repeat of the situation in 1914.

With clinical efficiency, the German armies blitzkrieged their way across western Poland so that when on 17 September, the Russian Red Army joined the invasion of that country from the east, the fate of the Polish people was sealed. The initial success of the German forces was spectacular. Hitler's armies comprised the new inventory for modern warfare – fast-moving, heavily armoured Panzers, motorised infantry, crack paratroopers – all superbly trained and equipped and supported by Heinkels, Messerschmitts and screeching Stuka dive-bombers that were said to be the 'flying artillery' of the *Luftwaffe*.

The conquest of Poland completed, Hitler embarked on a 'peace offensive', claiming that he had no further territorial claims in mind. During this time all was quiet along the Western Front so that people spoke of a 'Sitzkrieg' or even a 'phoney war'. Finally, on 9 April 1940, Hitler's patience gave way as he set in motion Operation *Weser* and ordered his armies to strike northwards to occupy Denmark and Norway. Landings took place by sea and air and, although the Allies sent a force to help the Norwegians, the operation was badly mishandled and by the end of May the country had to be abandoned to the Nazis. On 10 May, the German offensive in the west began in earnest with the invasion of the Netherlands and Belgium. The situation deteriorated rapidly as the Dutch were overwhelmed and the Belgians were forced to retreat. From the Allied viewpoint, disaster followed disaster, as the German armies broke through in the Ardennes and their armour raced across Flanders to reach Abbeville at the mouth of the River Somme on 20 May and so completed the encirclement of the Allied armies in the north. There was no chance of a breakout by the beleaguered Allies and, in spite of heroically fought delaying actions, the Allies were gradually squeezed within a perimeter around Dunkirk which, by 28 May, was barely thirty-five miles deep and less than twenty miles wide. Circumstances brought about by a combination of a German error of judgement and

Daily Mail headline on Monday 4 September 1939 announces that Britain and France are at war with Germany.

A J. C. Walker cartoon in the *South Wales Echo* of 19 September 1939 depicts 'courageous' Poland under attack from both Nazi Germany and Soviet Russia.

unexpected good fortune, allowed the so-called 'miracle of Dunkirk' when Admiral Bertram Ramsay organised a fleet of assorted small ships to carry out an emergency evacuation. As a result of Operation *Dynamo*, over 224,000 men of the BEF were rescued from the beaches as well as 141,000 other Allied servicemen, mostly French.

On 28 May, Belgium surrendered and, in face of a major German offensive, the demoralized French armies fell apart. With a German victory in the west virtually assured, Mussolini's Italy declared war on France and Britain. By this time, Paris was under threat from a German pincer movement and, to save the capital from possible destruction, the French commander-in-chief declared it an 'open city'. On 16 June, the Cabinet of Paul Reynaud fell and, to face the mounting crisis, the eighty-four-year-old former 'hero of Verdun', Marshal Pétain, was appointed prime minister. 'Armistice is inevitable,' he said; 'it should be requested without delay.'

On 22 June, a German delegation led by Hitler himself finally received the surrender of France. The Führer arranged for it to be signed at Compiègne in the very same railway carriage that was used in November 1918 when the defeated Germans accepted terms for an armistice. The French commander-in-chief, General Maxine Weygand, maintained that, with Russia in alliance with Germany, and the United States unwilling to intervene, it would only be a matter of time before Britain 'had her neck wrung like a chicken'.

The *Daily Express* of 31 May 1940 gives details of the BEF being brought home 'in history's strongest armada'.

The 'British Government's Grief and Amazement' at the French decision to sign an armistice is reported in the *Sunday Dispatch* of 23 June 1940.

Even as the last remnants of the British Expeditionary Force were being brought home from the beaches of Dunkirk, Winston Churchill gave the following notice: 'Britain will fight on ... If necessary for years ... If necessary alone ... We shall go back.' It was to be four long years to the month before Allied armies would return to France to begin the struggle for the liberation of their country.

First Britain had to survive herself. As Hitler threatened invasion and warned, 'Since England, in spite of her military hopeless position, shows no signs of coming to terms, I have decided to prepare a landing operation against England', so Churchill's government made arrangements to evacuate children, recruit a civilian army, which became known as the Home Guard, and organize the nation's defences. Of course, Britain was not truly alone during the period which Churchill referred to as her 'finest hour'. Since the outbreak of war, servicemen from the Commonwealth had been arriving to help defend the 'mother country' and these were now reinforced by those who had escaped from German-occupied Europe, determined to carry on the fight from Britain. In addition, while the United States remained neutral, President Franklin D. Roosevelt declared that his country 'must be the great arsenal of democracy' and saw to it that vital war supplies were made available, firstly under a Cash and Carry scheme and then under Lend-Lease. During the months of the Battle of Britain (July-October 1940), the German *Luftwaffe* failed to win mastery of the skies, which the German leader saw as an essential prerequisite to the invasion of the island. Smarting at the loss of 1,733 aircraft during the twelve-week battle and deprived of air superiority, he was forced to revise his plans. Operation *Sealion*, the planned invasion of England, was called off and instead Hitler ordered the indiscriminate bombing of British towns and cities.

The *Daily Mail* of 16 September 1940 boasts the 'Greatest Day for RAF'. In fact the claim that 175 German aircraft were shot down was an exaggeration, the real figure was only 76. The RAF lost 55 aircraft – 34 shot down and 21 destroyed on the ground.

Even more important, the German Führer decided to embark on Operation *Barbarossa* and on 22 June 1941 German forces began the invasion of Soviet Russia. With Hungary, Romania and Finland joining the Axis, German successes continued as their armies advanced deep into Russia to threaten Leningrad and Moscow and raced across the Ukraine as they headed towards the oil-rich Caucasus.

Elsewhere, the Germans invaded Yugoslavia and Greece and, although the British sent help, they were driven from both the Greek mainland and the island of Crete. In North Africa, the Allies did gain some limited success during a series of seesaw campaigns until the summer of 1942 when they were finally chased out of Libya by Rommel's Afrika Korps. With Alexandria and the Suez Canal threatened, the British Eighth Army finally made a stand at El Alamein.

Earlier, on 7 December 1941, a date that Roosevelt said 'will live in infamy', the Japanese attacked the American naval base at Pearl Harbour. Once Germany and Italy had declared war on the United States, what had been a European conflict now assumed global proportions. The American involvement rapidly transformed the situation. Backed by that nation's resources in both men and materials, the Soviet Union, Britain and their Allies were able to step up the war against the Axis powers and, slowly but

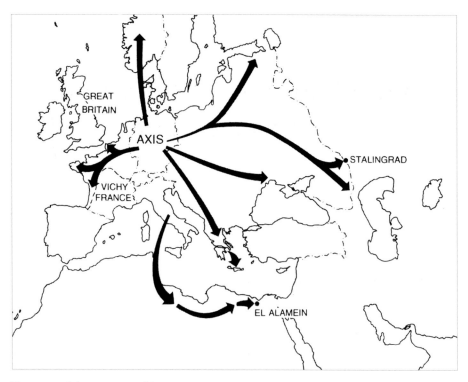

The extent of the expansion of the Axis powers across Europe and North Africa before the reversals at El Alamein (October 1942) and Stalingrad (January 1943).

surely, the tide began to turn. First it was the British at El Alamein who won a resounding victory over Rommel's Afrika Korps in October 1942 then, three months later, in January 1943, the Russians encircled von Paulus's German armies at Stalingrad and forced them to surrender. As Churchill later boasted, 'Before Alamein we never had a victory. After Alamein we never had a defeat.'

Along the length of the Eastern Front, the Russians had suffered massive losses as they bore the brunt of the German onslaught. Stalin urged the Western Allies to bring some relief by opening a 'second front'. The British and Americans were, of course, heavily involved elsewhere – in the Far East against the Japanese and in North Africa. Once the surrender of the Axis forces in Africa had been brought about in May 1943, they began the invasion of the 'soft underbelly' of Europe, first Sicily and then Italy. Still, an invasion in the north-west would come, it was just a matter of time, and of where, and of when ...

2

FRANCE UNDER OCCUPATION – THE RESISTANCE

On 14 June 1940, as German troops were about to enter Paris, the French government moved to Bordeaux. By this time rumour and confusion had created some considerable misunderstanding and mistrust between the British and French authorities and this was soon to be further aggravated by German propaganda. Many Frenchmen felt they had been left in the lurch by the British and there were rumours that French soldiers had been abandoned on the beaches at Dunkirk. It was also thought that the British Expeditionary Force (BEF) had been both too small and ineffective and that the RAF had not been fully committed but held in reserve in readiness to defend the British mainland.

One French general, Charles de Gaulle, made a dramatic escape to Britain. From London he broadcast to the French people – '*La flamme de la Resistance française ne doit pas s'éteindre et ne s'éteindra pas.*' Soon afterwards, in a printed proclamation, he declared '*La France a perdu une bataille, mais elle n'a pas perdu la guerre.*'

The terms of the armistice were agreed and accepted by Petain and his pro-Nazi henchman, Pierre Laval. Alsace and Lorraine were once again to become a part of Germany while the remainder of France was to be divided into occupied and unoccupied zones. The Germans were to occupy the north and the full extent of the Atlantic coast while the remainder, the interior and the Mediterranean coast, was to remain under the control of Petain's government.

France was to pay the costs of the occupation. The French army was to be disarmed and demobilised while prisoners-of-war held by the Germans would not be released until the war was over – that was, until Britain had been defeated.

On area of major concern for the British was the future of the French fleet. Unwilling to take a chance that it might fall into the hands of the Germans, Churchill authorised Operation *Catapult* in which the Royal Navy was dispatched to sink French battleships based in North African ports. Some 1,300 French sailors were killed, which soured relations between the former allies even further and added weight to Nazi propaganda which claimed that, as usual, the British were only prepared to fight to the last Frenchman.

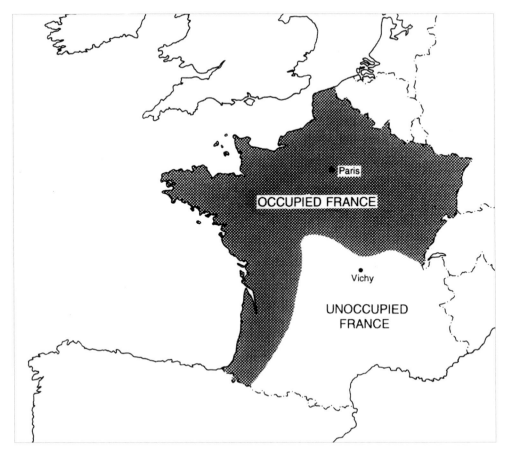

The division of France into occupied and unoccupied regions. Unoccupied France was generally known as Vichy France.

In Unoccupied France, Petain established his government at the spa town of Vichy and consequently the region became known as Vichy France. With a great many Frenchmen, Petain still remained very popular and attracted 'almost mystical adulation'. There was a feeling that he had saved France from an even worse fate. At a meeting with Hitler in Montoire in October 1940, the Vichy-French leader proclaimed, 'To maintain the unity of France within the New Order of Europe, I enter today upon a path of collaboration.' Collaboration meant working with the Nazis and agreeing to take measures against French Jews. As Hitler ordered the requisition of large quantities of raw materials and machinery, Vichy France became no more than a German puppet-state. The region's difficulties were increased by an influx of refugees and demobilised soldiers and so acute were the shortages that during the winter of 1940/41 many French families faced the threat of starvation. Across the country the Milice, a Gestapo-style police force made up of collaborators, watched over the people as the country was forced to accept the barbarism of Nazi rule. In spite of this, French national consciousness began to revive and a great many brave men and women refused to collaborate and instead organised themselves into Resistance groups. During the years of occupation thousands were tortured to death or shot.

In November 1942, Anglo-American forces carried out landings along the coast of French North Africa in Operation *Torch*. The Germans reacted to this by occupying the whole of France. Their hopes of seizing what was left of the French navy based at Toulon, however, were frustrated by Admiral Darlan who ordered the fleet to be scuttled.

In Occupied France there had always been some isolated resistance to the Germans but it was during the period between the summer of 1941 and June 1944 that organised resistance really developed. The German invasion of the Soviet Union in 1941 brought an increased commitment by French Communists who formed the backbone of the *Front Nationale* and *Libération-Nord*. Resistance became more general once the Germans began the compulsory deportation of French workers to serve as forced labour in German factories. Many Frenchmen avoided deportation by disappearing into the countryside where they formed Resistance groups known as the Maquis. It is said that some fifty thousand young Frenchmen became active Maquisards and their deeds became legendary.

In London, General de Gaulle had become the rallying-point for all Frenchmen determined to continue the fight against Germany. Using the Cross of Lorraine as his symbol, he formed a French National Committee and assumed the leadership of French servicemen in Britain, the Free French. From London, he managed to win over a number of French overseas territories to the Gaullist cause and, in the spring of 1943, a Free French government was set up in North Africa. Even so, the general did not get on well with the British – he had reservations about them and they in turn found him truculent and difficult. In France, some Resistance groups accepted de Gaulle's leadership but many did not. The Communists, who dominated the Resistance in many regions, distrusted him while other groups preferred to work independently. Eventually all the groups agreed to merge to form the FFI – French Forces of the Interior. After May 1941, the activities of the French Resistance were assisted by the British SOE (Special Operations Executive). This organisation, whose aim, said Churchill, 'was to set Europe ablaze', supplied arms and equipment, used Lysander aircraft to land its agents in France and is best remembered for the heroism of its members such as Violette Szabo, Harry Ree, Odette Sansom, Nora Khan, Albert Guerisse, Edward Yeo-Thomas and a great many others. More than 130 men and women lost their lives during secret operations in France.

Resistance took many forms – listening to the forbidden BBC, anti-German graffiti operating clandestine printing presses, running escape routes for Allied aircrew, organising demonstrations and strikes, carrying out widespread acts of sabotage which disrupted communications and damaged essential industries as well as a host of other guerrilla activities.

Membership of the Resistance was always precarious, with the chance of betrayal, capture, torture and death. After the German takeover of Vichy France, all sections of the Resistance movement came under the *Conseil National de la Résistance*, before de Gaulle was finally accepted as the undisputed leader, when the *Comité Français de Libération Nationale* was formed to take overall responsibility for its organisation. Preceded by the opening bars of Beethoven's Fifth Symphony (V for Victory), each night a stream of coded messages and instructions – *messages personnels* – were sent from London on the BBC's French service.

By the start of 1944, there were over 100,000 Frenchmen actively involved with the Resistance. During the months before D-Day they managed to destroy over 1,800 railway locomotives, paralyse large sections of the French railway system and openly harass the movement of German units. In March 1944 at Glières, 500 Maquisards held eight thousand Germans, well supported by tanks and aircraft, for several days. In 1944, the creation of the *Forces Françaises de l'Intérieur* (FFI) meant that the activities of the French Resistance became directly integrated with the Allied invasion plans. Throughout the early summer of 1944, France was abuzz with espionage activity and this meant that, as the Germans made their preparations to defend their European fortress against the forthcoming Allied invasion, they also had to be very mindful of their backs.

When the time came, the French Resistance was to play its part in the liberation of their homeland, often at a very heavy cost. Shortly after D-Day, the *SS Das Reich Panzer Division*, which had been ordered to move from Toulouse to Normandy, was so effectively harassed by the Resistance that it was delayed by over ten days. On the 10 June, and as an act of reprisal, men of that unit massacred the entire population of the village of Oradour-sur-Glane near Limoges. Not only did 642 villagers perish but afterwards their homes were burned and gutted. During the following month, some three thousand Resistance fighters raised the Tricolour on the Vercors plateau, a mountainous region to the south-west of Grenoble. They fought magnificently for over five weeks but were gradually overwhelmed by the Germans. Once again, the SS subjected the Frenchmen to their retribution. Not even the wounded and prisoners were spared as over seven hundred survivors were systematically slaughtered. It is said that during this period the value of the French Resistance was equal to ten divisions of regular troops.

3

GERMAN PLANS TO DEFEND 'FESTUNG EUROPA' – THEIR EUROPEAN FORTRESS

Although the German high command was well aware that the Allies were planning to invade in the West, they could only guess where and when the blow would fall. They had about three thousand miles of coastline to watch over from the French Atlantic coast to the Low Countries, but then it might be Norway or possibly somewhere along the Riviera. Even when Allied fortunes had been at a low ebb, the Germans had been subject to pin-prick, hit-and-run commando raids which may have had little strategic value but certainly gave a boost to British morale. As early as the summer of 1940, there had been raids on the French coast and the Channel Islands. In March 1941 came the first large-scale commando assault on the Lofoten Islands off the coast of Norway and this was followed in August by landings at Spitzbergen. In February 1942 paratroopers of the 1st Airborne Division destroyed the radio-location site at Bruneval, just twelve miles to the north-east of Le Havre, and this was followed a month later by the destruction of the gates of the dry dock at St Nazaire, built some ten years earlier to accommodate the French liner *Normandie*. Then in August 1942 came disaster – the raid on Dieppe.

The aim of the raid on the French coastal resort was to gain first-hand experience of invasion tactics by making an opposed landing. Opposed it certainly was and of the 6,100 men who took part, mainly drawn from the 4th and 6th Canadian Infantry Brigades and the 14th Canadian Army Tank Brigade, some 3,648 were killed, wounded, missing or taken prisoner. With some justification, the Germans gloated over their success and the *Münchner Neueste Nachricaten* commented, 'Dieppe has enriched us by much precious experience ... Dieppe has shown that the German rampart on the Atlantic coast is up to all tests.' While the raid was not a full-scale invasion attempt, as the Germans suggested, it made the Allies more acutely aware of the difficulties of landing on a fortified beach and against organised opposition.

Some Germans considered the most likely choice for an Allied invasion would be somewhere along the Pas de Calais, when only thirty-four kilometres of the English Channel separated the British and French coastlines, but they were also aware that the Allies had other options. They might attempt ploys such as beginning with a diversionary landing in one area before the major invasion force landed in another or carrying out simultaneous landings at different places.

As early as 1941, Hitler had given instructions for 'the construction of a new West Wall to assure protection of the Arctic, North Sea and Atlantic coasts'. In order to repel an invasion, the Germans built coastal defences of massive proportions – the so-called 'Atlantic Wall'. Consisting of bunkers, pillboxes, strongpoints and gun emplacements, its construction, which was started in 1942, required some 13.2 million cubic metres of concrete and 1.3 million tonnes of steel. The work was done mainly be foreign labourers and Russian and Polish prisoners-of-war forcibly recruited into the slave-labour organisation run by the German construction engineer, Fritz Todt. In addition, the beaches at most likely landing sites were reinforced with barbed wire, minefields, and tank and underwater obstacles while, inland, fields were spiked with 'Rommel's asparagus' – poles placed in the ground to make glider landings even more hazardous. The 'Wall' was built in greatest depth between Cap Gris Nez and Boulogne. The defence of the coastline fell to the men of the *Wehrmacht* supported by five powerful Panzer divisions equipped with Tigers – the most heavily armoured of all German tanks. The overall command of '*Festung Europa*' (Fortress Europe) was entrusted to Field Marshal Karl von Rundstedt.

The sixty-nine-year old aristocrat was a long-serving professional soldier who had retired before the outbreak of war. Ordered back to active service, he had already proved his worth during the successful German offensive in France in 1940 and on the Eastern Front during 1940-41. He had the proud reputation of having never lost a battle. Still, it was his criticisms of Hitler's campaign strategy in Russia which had led to his removal to France and now, in the summer of 1944, he lived in a splendid château overlooking the River Seine at St Germaine-en-Laye. He had no illusions about his task and saw it as near impossible. Later he noted, 'I have over three thousand miles of coastline to cover … and over sixty divisions with which to defend it.' Of the Atlantic Wall, he said 'The Wall was a myth, nothing in front of it, nothing behind – a mere showpiece.'

German *armeegruppe* B, which consisted of the 7th Army in Normandy and Brittany and the 15th Army deployed further to the east, was under the command of Field Marshal Erwin Rommel, an imaginative and much respected general already famous for his exploits with the Afrika Korps in the North African desert. Rommel was not at all impressed with the quality of the coastal defences. He quickly identified the areas of greatest vulnerability and at his direction they were strengthened. Von Rundstedt and Rommel were not ideal partners since they differed in background, temperament and in their concepts of tactical planning.

Von Rundstedt intended to hold his Panzers well back until the invaders were established ashore and then use them in a massive counter-attack intended to drive the Allies back into the sea. Rommel, on the other hand, was convinced that the first twenty-four hours of the invasion would be the most crucial. He calculated that Allied air attacks would easily destroy Panzer tank formations held in reserve and thought it imperative that they were used immediately to strike at the invaders as they came ashore. The issue was put to Hitler who had by now deprived his generals of the right to use their own initiative and assumed command of all German armies in both East and West himself. The Führer had some sympathy with Rommel's point of view but he decided on a compromise – some of the Panzers would be put in forward positions and some held back. He also placed all Panzer divisions under his own personal control. In fact, the location of these units was to be of great importance during the period immediately following the Allied landings on the 6 June. The basis of Rommel's whole defence strategy depended on him having the means to strike at the enemy while they were still on the beaches and before they had established a bridgehead but he faced many other problems. The German general had to cope with shortages of both men and materials. He lacked adequate supplies of cement to complete his system of coastal fortifications, he estimated that he needed fifty million mines for use as the basis of his beach defences but received only six million and his system of transport was becoming increasingly dependent on horse-drawn vehicles. He also knew that he had little with which to challenge the aerial supremacy of the Allies.

Although there were Panzers and other élite units of the German army stationed in France, few of the men detailed to defend the 'Atlantic Wall' were battle-hardened. The *Wehrmacht* was bolstered by regiments of *Osttruppen*, which were made up of volunteers drawn from the occupied countries, particularly Ukrainians, Georgians and other Russian nationalities. There were also a number of units consisting of invalids transferred to the West after fighting on the Eastern Front.

By the early summer of 1944, the signs of an imminent Allied invasion were becoming increasingly obvious. There were continuous Allied troop movements and activity as men and materials were massed along the south coast of England. There was a significant increase in Allied air attacks on strategic targets in Northern France while the French Resistance became more active and acts of sabotage multiplied. Of course, German Intelligence knew what was going on but were powerless to prevent it. Hitler had underestimated the strength of the Allied invasion forces and was unaware that the Allies were constructing artificial harbours for use once the invasion started. The once great *Luftwaffe* was now rarely seen and this allowed the RAF and USAAF complete mastery in the skies. At sea, the German Navy was in no position to challenge a cross-Channel invasion.

To face the onslaught when it came, Rommel's armeegruppe B had forty-three divisions covering the coast from Normandy to Holland. One of these, the 19th Panzer Division, was being refitted after being severely mauled on the Eastern Front while another, the 319th Infantry Division, was in the Channel Islands. The bulk of the Normandy coastline was to be defended by the VII Armee commanded by General Friedrich Dollmann while to the east, beyond the River Orne, lay General Hans von

Salmuth's XV Armee. To the west, along the Cotentin Peninsula, were the 243rd and 709th Infantry Divisions while between the River Dives and River Merderet and close to Carentan was the 91st Division with the 6th Parachute Regiment held in reserve. Along the main length of the Normandy coast between the River Vire and the River Orne, the 352nd and 716th Infantry Divisions stood guard while the area immediately to the east and beyond the River Orne was allocated to 771st Infantry Division which was part of von Salmuth's XV Armee. Close to Caen was the 21st Panzer Division and to the south the crack Panzer Lehr Division. The fanatical teenagers of the 12th SS (*Hitler Jugend*) Panzer Division were close to St Lô. Rommel well knew that these, his best units, could only be committed to battle by Hitler himself. On D-Day, it would be the 709th, 352nd and 716th Infantry Divisions which would face the first Allied assaults along the Normandy coastline. To the east, there were large concentrations of German forces in the region of the Pas de Calais where von Rundstedt was still convinced the main blow would fall. There is some irony in the fact that in May 1944 Hitler accurately forecast that the invasion would take place in Normandy. It was the Allies' good fortune that he refused to back his intuition and, instead, agreed to compromise once more.

4

THE BUILD-UP TO D-DAY

The liberation of Nazi-occupied Europe began long before D-Day. By June 1944, the Soviet armies had followed up their successes at Stalingrad (January 1943) and Kursk (July 1943) by liberating most of the Ukraine so that in Eastern Europe they were now pressing close to the frontiers of Poland, Hungary and Rumania. With all Axis forces cleared from North Africa, on 10 July 1943 Allied forces under General Dwight D. Eisenhower began Operation *Husky* – the invasion of Sicily. By mid-August, the British 8th Army commanded by General Sir Bernard Montgomery and the US 7th Army under General George Patton had overrun the island. With the invasion of Italy imminent, Mussolini was forced to resign and was imprisoned. Although he was later rescued by German airborne troops, his effective rule as the Fascist dictator of Italy was over. On 3 September 1943, British and American forces crossed the Straits of Messina to begin the invasion of Italy. After three long years Allied forces were once again on mainland Europe. Naples fell early in October 1943 and, shortly afterwards, Italy changed course and entered the war on the Allied side. With torrential rain making the going difficult, Allied troops began a protracted winter struggle as they fought their way forward against German defensive positions in the Apennines. In fact, Rome was not reached until 4 June, two days before D-Day, and German resistance in Italy continued until May 1945. At the end of December 1943 both Eisenhower and Montgomery were recalled to London where they were to be involved in the planning of the next stage of the war, the invasion of Western Europe.

From Britain, RAF Bomber Command and the United States 8th Air Force had stepped up their strategic bombing offensive against Germany and thousand-bomber raids against German industrial centres had become commonplace. It was some measure of the destruction that German civilian casualties due to Allied bombing totalled some 600,000 – nearly ten times the British losses during the blitz! Much of Bomber Command success was the result of the development of a long-range escort fighter, the Mustang, which provided Allied bombers, with much needed fighter cover against the *Luftwaffe*. Although the bombing campaign had some considerable impact, German war production was far from crippled. It would not, as some Allied strategists believed, bring about an end to the war in itself. The need to open a second front was now even more imperative.

In the United States, some sections of American public opinion had pressed for a maximum effort to be made to deal with Japan first but President Roosevelt would have none of this. Even though it was now agreed that the liberation of Western Europe would come first, many Americans were critical that the British seemed only half-hearted in their support for a cross-Channel invasion and still preferred a Mediterranean-based strategy. It was at the Casablanca Conference in January 1943 that the planning of the invasion started in earnest. Up to that point, Churchill and Roosevelt had held differing views – the British prime minister pressed for an all-out invasion along the coast of northern France while the American president put forward the idea of a two-pronged invasion with simultaneous landings in the north and the south along the French Riviera. It was finally accepted that Roosevelt's plan would over extend Allied resources and that the projected invasion of southern France would be best deferred until a month or so after D-Day.

To begin with, the overall planning of the Allied invasion of northern France, Operation *Overlord*, was left to a team led by Lieutenant General Sir Frederick Morgan, who was Chief of Staff to the Supreme Allied Commander – a post yet to be filled. The team, made up of both British and American senior staff, was known as COSSAC. In spite of differences of opinion between the British and Americans and inter-service rivalries, plans for the massive combined operations undertaking gradually took shape. The COSSAC planners envisaged an initial landing on the Normandy coast, the immediate capture of essential ports and, once a build-up had been completed, an advance inland. They decided that immediate supplies would be made available through the construction of artificial harbours, which would be towed across the Channel, and that fuel supplies would be maintained by a direct pipeline to the invasion beaches. The date set for the operation was 1 May 1944.

The appointment of a Supreme Allied Commander was a sensitive issue. The British had been involved in the war for five years but the Americans would be making the largest contribution of men and materials. The final choice was Eisenhower. Nicknamed 'Ike', General Dwight D. Eisenhower was a Texan. He graduated from West Point in 1915 and during the Great War was mainly engaged in home-based training. At the start of the Second World War, he was still only a lieutenant-colonel but promotion came fast. In February 1943, he was appointed general and in November of that year he was appointed to command the Allied invasion of French North Africa. Eisenhower was an amiable and much-liked man. His great gifts were his organisational abilities and his tactful management of those under his command. He was liked by the British and was considered the man best able to reconcile any differences between members of his Anglo-American team. His deputy was to be Air Chief Marshal Sir Arthur Tedder, an RAF man and former Commander of Allied Air Forces in the Mediterranean. During the Great War, Tedder had been an infantry subaltern and served on the Western Front until he transferred to the Royal Flying Corps in 1916. Three other senior positions also fell to British officers. Although Eisenhower expressed a preference for General Harold Alexander, he had to accept the more tetchy General Sir Bernard Montgomery as Commander in Chief of Allied Ground Forces. 'Monty', as he was affectionately known by British servicemen, had served in the trenches during the Great War and had participated in the Dunkirk evacuation in 1940. He was a difficult, self-opinionated man but his military record spoke for itself. He had revived the flagging spirits of the men of the British Eighth Army and then led them to victory over Rommel's Afrika Korps at El Alamein in October 1942. He successfully breached the Mareth Line in March 1943 and, after the Axis forces had been driven from North Africa, took part in the invasions of Sicily and Italy. Admiral Sir Bertram Ramsay, who had earlier planned the Dunkirk evacuation and the Allied invasion of French North Africa, was to be Naval Commander in Chief. Sadly he was to be killed in an air crash before the end of the war. Air Marshal Sir Trafford Leigh-Mallory, who had been a fighter-group commander during the Battle of Britain, was given responsibility for Allied air operations. Thought to be scheming, indecisive and unduly pessimistic, he was the subject of much personal antipathy. He too died in an air crash before the end of the war. The team was completed with two Americans, the much-liked 'Brad' – Lieutenant General Omar Bradley – and Eisenhower's Chief-of-Staff, Lieutenant General Walter Bedell Smith.

COSSAC was now replaced by SHAEF, Supreme Headquarters Allied Expeditionary Force, and Eisenhower set up his headquarters at Bushey Park in the outskirts of London. It rapidly developed into a canvas village and was known as 'Widewing'. Other operations centres were established at Stanmore and Southwick Park near Portsmouth.

The plan put forward by Montgomery was very different from those originally suggested by COSSAC. He wanted the invasion front broadened so that the Americans would land along the east coast of the Contenin Peninsula while the British and Canadians would go ashore further to the east on the beaches extending towards the River Orne. The flanks of the designated invasion area were to be protected by airborne landings. Once the bridgeheads had been established and developed, the British and Canadians would contain the bulk of the German armour and so allow the Americans to break out to the west, take Cherbourg, advance into Brittany and southwards towards the River Loire. The extent of the operations would make it necessary to increase the size of the assault force from three to five divisions. Montgomery's proposals were approved and the invasion date set for early June.

Training and exercises in readiness for D-Day had been going on since early 1943. In May 1944, a series of staged rehearsals code-named Fabius were carried out along the south coast in areas where the beaches were similar to those to be found in Normandy. Off Slapton Sands, to the east of Dartmouth in Devon, German E-boats interrupted an

American exercise and succeeded in sinking a number of landing craft. Altogether some seven hundred US servicemen lost their lives. In addition to British troops, many of them veterans recalled from Italy and other theatres of war, the country became a vast assembly area for nearly two million US servicemen, Canadians and others from the Commonwealth as well as smaller contingents from the occupied countries – men from France, Belgium, Poland, Czechoslovakia, Denmark, Norway and the Netherlands. Once the invasion got under way, fliers from Australia, New Zealand, South Africa and Rhodesia would play their part with the RAF and USAAF in helping to destroy German communications and harassing Panzer columns and the movement of German reserves and supplies towards the forward areas. By April, as preparations for D-Day neared completion, the south of England became a veritable armed camp. Relations between the GIs and the local population were generally good, though some grew jealous of their lifestyle and expressed the view that the Americans were 'overpaid, overfed, oversexed and over here'. The US authorities went as far as to issue a special booklet intended to help their servicemen better understand the British temperament and way of life!

With D-Day approaching, the planners became more aware than ever before of the importance of the wartime slogan 'Careless talk costs lives'. German agents were still active in the country and, across the Irish Sea, walked freely into the streets of Dublin. Security had to be strict and civilian movement curtailed. Military contact with the civilian population was discouraged and identity cards were frequently and rigidly checked. Allied intelligence played its part by keeping the enemy guessing with feints and deceptions intended to mislead the Germans. Fake tanks and landing craft were openly displayed in Kent opposite the Pas de Calais and well away from the areas where the real preparations were being made.

Along the coast, hidden in bays and inlets, were the sections of concrete breakwaters and steel pontoons which were soon to be floated across the Channel to form the all-important artificial Mulberry harbours. The idea of a submarine oil pipeline, PLUTO (the Pipe Line Under the Ocean) had already been tested between Swansea and Ilfracombe and, when it was feasible, it would be laid between the Isle of Wight and Cherbourg.

Allied planning had been meticulous. Old holiday snaps and postcards had been collected and studied together with tide-tables and the evidence of aerial photography. Much useful information was supplied by the French Resistance regarding the whereabouts and strength of the German defences while mini-submarines went close inshore and actually landed men to check on the nature of the sand and carry out beach surveys. The Allied commanders knew that the Normandy beaches were bristling with mines and other obstructions and that these would have to be cleared before the main landing forces could make their way ashore. To help deal with this, General Montgomery's brother-in-law, Major General Percy Hobart of the 79th Armoured Division, had quite brilliantly adapted tanks to perform a range of extraordinary functions. Known as 'Hobart's Funnies', they included 'swimming tanks', amphibious tanks which floated on skirts and were powered by propellers; and 'flail tanks', known as 'Crabs', which carried chain flails attached to rotating drums that detonated mines lying in their path. He also developed carpet-laying or 'Bobbin tanks' which carried a roll of canvas that could be unwound and placed across soft sand to provide a more stable road surface; 'Crocodile tanks', much dreaded by the Germans, which were equipped with flame throwers that could spew out a jet of fire a hundred metres ahead; 'Fascine tanks' which carried bundles of wooden palings that could be used to fill holes; tanks specifically designed to destroy strongpoints by hurling large 'flying dustbin shells'; and tanks that could be used to rescue disabled tanks.

From late May until the beginning of June, convoys of military vehicles had streamed south taking men and equipment the assembly areas. Four days before D-Day, then set for Monday 5 June, the invasion forces to be used in the initial assault were sealed off in closely guarded embarkation areas. As men boarded their ships so their officers received their final briefings. The weather was bad and with meteorologists predicting high winds and rough seas, Montgomery was still prepared to go but Eisenhower waited for as long as he dared before deciding to delay the operation for twenty-four hours in the hope that conditions would improve. The excitement meant that, although the strain on the men increased, their morale remained high. At headquarters at Southwick House overlooking Portsmouth, Sunday 4 June proved a tense and uncertain day for the planners. By the morning of the 5 June, the Winds had not really abated but the forecast was better. Eisenhower had to make the decision. Many men had been confined to their boats for days and some were already at sea but more important was the fact that the tides along the Normandy beaches would soon change and a further delay might mean cancellation. Out to sea, conditions, although still unpleasant, were beginning to ease. 'I don't like it, but there it is ... I don't see how we can possibly do anything else.' The decision had been made – Operation *Overlord* was to go ahead.

5

OPERATION *OVERLORD* –
D-DAY, 6 JUNE 1944

Area 'Z', the assembly area for the invasion armada, was mid-Channel just to the south-east of the Isle of Wight. During the afternoon of Monday 5 June, seven thousand vessels carrying 130,000 men and their equipment headed for that rendezvous point. The sea was still rough and the issue of sea-sickness tablets did little to alleviate the discomfort of the men on the bobbing craft. In fact, the bad weather conditions allowed an even greater element of surprise since the German high command thought an invasion would be impossible in such circumstances. The high seas meant that German patrol ships remained in port and the inclement weather made radar installations largely ineffective. Once the invasion started, it would be supported by twelve thousand Allied aircraft against which the Germans could muster less than five hundred. The invading forces all formed part of the 21st Army Group (General Sir Bernard Montgomery). It consisted of the US First Army (Lieutenant General Omar Bradley) and the British Second Army (Lieutenant General Sir Miles Dempsey). The US First Army was comprised of the VIIth Corps (Major General J. Lawton Collins) and Vth Corps (Major General Léonard T. Gerow) while the British Second Army was made up of XXXth Corps (Lieutenant General G.C. Bucknall) and 1st Corps (Lieutenant General J. T. Crocker).

The invasion area along the Normandy coastline had been divided into five landing areas – two American, Utah and Omaha; two British, Gold and Sword; and, between the British beaches, one Canadian, Juno. Each beach was further divided into sectors. The troops of the US 4th Division were to land on Utah at the base of the Cotentin Peninsula while the US 29th and 1st Divisions were to storm ashore on Omaha.

The British and Canadian beaches were to the east of the American with Port-en-Bessin the approximate dividing line. The British 50th Infantry Division was to land on Gold, the Canadian 3rd Infantry Division on Juno and the British 3rd Infantry on Sword. Each was to be supported by an Armoured Brigade. The flanks of the seaborne landing area were to be protected by earlier airborne landings. In the west, the US 82nd and

---

Overleaf: Assembly of Allied Forces for the D-Day invasion

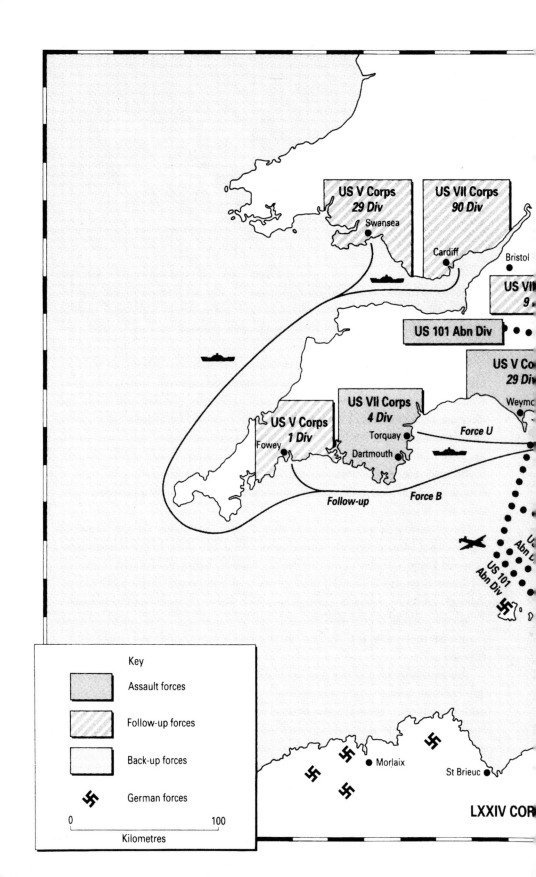

Key

Assault forces

Follow-up forces

Back-up forces

German forces

0 —————————— 100
Kilometres

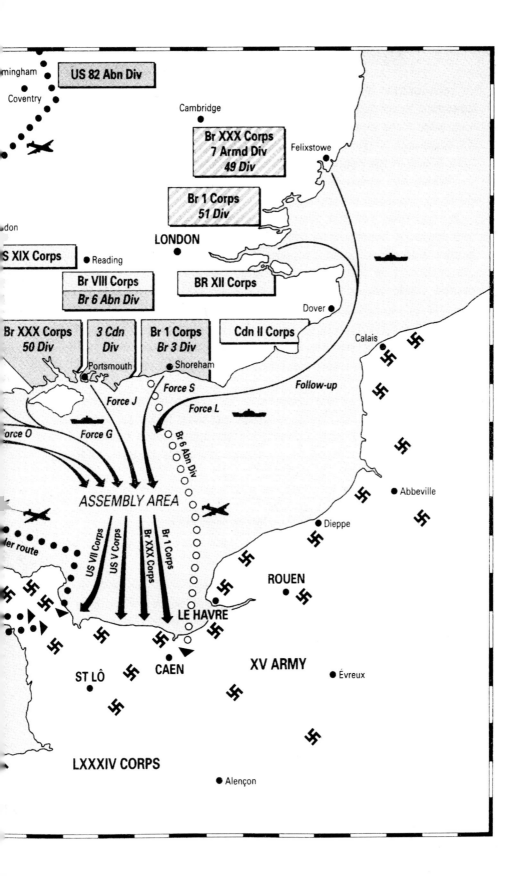

US 82 Abn Div

Cambridge

Br XXX Corps
7 Armd Div
49 Div

Felixstowe

Br 1 Corps
51 Div

LONDON

S XIX Corps • Reading

Br VIII Corps
Br 6 Abn Div

BR XII Corps

Dover

Br XXX Corps
50 Div

3 Cdn
Div

Br 1 Corps
Br 3 Div

Cdn II Corps

Calais

Portsmouth

Shoreham

Force S

Force J

Force L

Follow-up

orce O

Force G

Br 6 Abn Div

ASSEMBLY AREA

der route

US VII Corps

US V Corps

Br XXX Corps

Br 1 Corps

Abbeville

Dieppe

ROUEN

LE HAVRE

ST LÔ

CAEN

XV ARMY

Évreux

LXXXIV CORPS

Alençon

101st Airborne Divisions were to land close to the rear of Utah Beach in the region of the Rivers Merderet and Douve; in the east, the British 6th Airborne Division was to drop close to the bridges over the Caen Canal and River Orne.

The intention was that, after an intense sea and aerial bombardment, formations of landing craft would head for the beaches protected by gunfire from destroyers and support ships. The first engineer detachment ashore would be accompanied by amphibious tanks. Once these had cleared a path across the beaches, the main assault troops would land from LCAs – assault landing craft. These would then return to the troop transports and continue to shuttle to and fro between the beach and the troopships until the operation was complete. In the rough seas, movement down the side of the transports into the landing craft was hazardous in the extreme.

The landings along the coast were to be timed according to the sequence of high tides. However, before the main beach landings were attempted, US and British paratroopers and glider-borne troops had to land at the western and eastern extremities of the five designated landing areas.

THE INITIAL AIRBORNE LANDINGS

THE AMERICANS TO THE WEST

Ahead of the major American airborne landing due at 1.30 a.m. on the morning of D-Day, pathfinders were dropped to mark the limits of the landing zone. Then came the thirteen thousand men of the US 82nd Airborne Division under Major General Matthew Ridgway, and the US 101st Airborne Division under Major General Maxwell Taylor.

Their prime purpose was to secure the narrow causeways running across the flooded ground immediately to the rear of Utah Beach and hold bridges over the Rivers Meredet and Douve. Things did not go according to plan. The approach to the dropping zones followed an indirect route which made navigation difficult and, near to their target, the aircraft ran into cloud and German anti-aircraft fire. While some of the US 82nd Airborne Division landed on target, others came down in the flooded marshlands close to the two rivers. Many got into difficulty and quite a number drowned. They also unexpectedly landed in an area garrisoned by the German 91st *Luftlande* Division. The landing of the US 101st Division was scattered over a wide area so that many became lost. As a result of the confusion, the Division first found itself able to muster barely 20 per cent of its strength. In spite of this, Ste Mère-Église was in American hands by 4 a.m. and, at dawn, the important causeways behind Utah Beach were also under their control.

THE BRITISH TO THE EAST

The first gliders of Major General Gale's British 6th Airborne Division landed with amazing accuracy close to the bridge at Bénouville which spanned the Caen Canal – later famously called 'Pegasus Bridge'. Major John Howard's men took this and the bridge over the River Orne which was a short distance away. Other units attacked the German battery at Merville or set out to limit the scale of any immediate German counter-blow by destroying the various bridges over the River Dives and its tributaries. At 5 a.m. the main force of British paratroopers and glider-borne troops landed close to Ranville. This was only the start: ferocious fighting was to continue on the east bank of the River Orne for some weeks and prove costly to both sides.

At 3 a.m. the softening-up process prior to the seaborne landings began when 1,300 Allied bombers started to attack the German positions around the five designated landing areas. Afterwards the same stretch of coastline received a severe pounding from the guns of British and American battleships out to sea. The first ashore were the Americans at Utah.

THE SEABORNE LANDINGS

UTAH BEACH

The Americans landed at Utah Beach at 6.30 a.m. They were men of the 8th Regimental Combat Team of the US 4th Infantry Division, the leading division of General Lawton Collins's US VIIth Corps. The landing met unexpectedly light opposition largely because the troops came ashore two kilometres away from their intended landing area where the defences were relatively weak. They secured the beach easily and were able to begin their build-up immediately. By mid-day they had started to move inland. On the day, the Division sustained fewer than two hundred casualties. Their main objective was to link up with the airborne forces inland and then advance to cut the main Carentan to Cherbourg road as the first stage towards isolating the Contenin Peninsula.

Between Utah Beach and the next American landing area at Omaha lay the estuaries of the Rivers Douve and Vire and, a little further to the east beyond Grandcamp-Maisy, a rocky promontory, the Pointe du Hoc. It fell to the US 2nd and 5th Ranger Battalions under Lieutenant Colonel James E. Rudder to scale the cliffs and silence the German coastal battery at the top. The Rangers did magnificently but, when they finally took the position, they discovered the guns of the battery were not in place.

Overleaf: The designated landing areas of the British, Canadian and US forces on D-Day

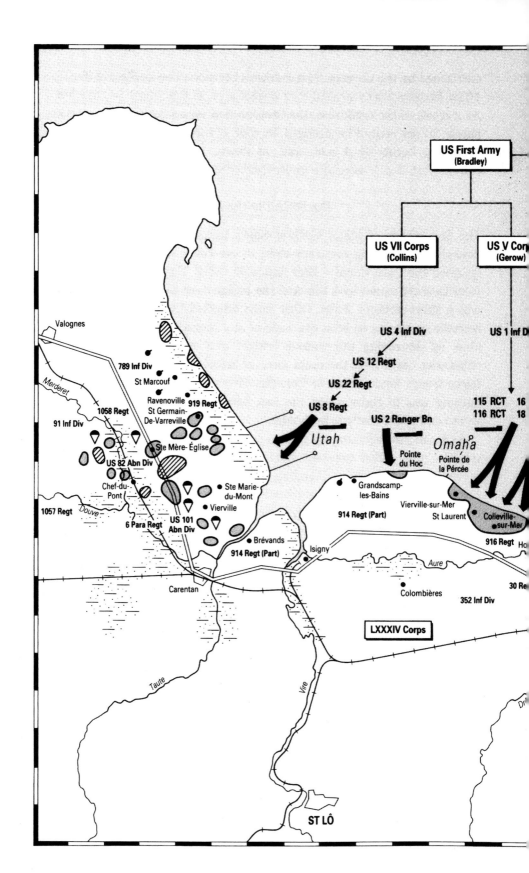

US First Army
(Bradley)

US VII Corps
(Collins)

US V Corps
(Gerow)

US 4 Inf Div

US 1 Inf Div

US 12 Regt

US 22 Regt

US 8 Regt

US 2 Ranger Bn

115 RCT   16
116 RCT   18

Utah

Omaha

Valognes

789 Inf Div

St Marcouf

Merderet

Ravenoville

919 Regt

St Germain-
De-Varreville

1058 Regt

91 Inf Div

Ste Mère- Église

US 82 Abn Div

Chef-du-
Pont

Pointe
du Hoc

Pointe de
la Pércée

Grandscamp-
les-Bains

Vierville-sur-Mer

St Laurent

Colleville-
sur-Mer

Ste Marie-
du-Mont

Vierville

1057 Regt

Douve

6 Para Regt

US 101
Abn Div

914 Regt (Part)

916 Regt   Ho

Brévands

Isigny

Aure

914 Regt (Part)

Carentan

Taute

Vire

Colombières

30 Re

352 Inf Div

LXXXIV Corps

ST LÔ

Dr

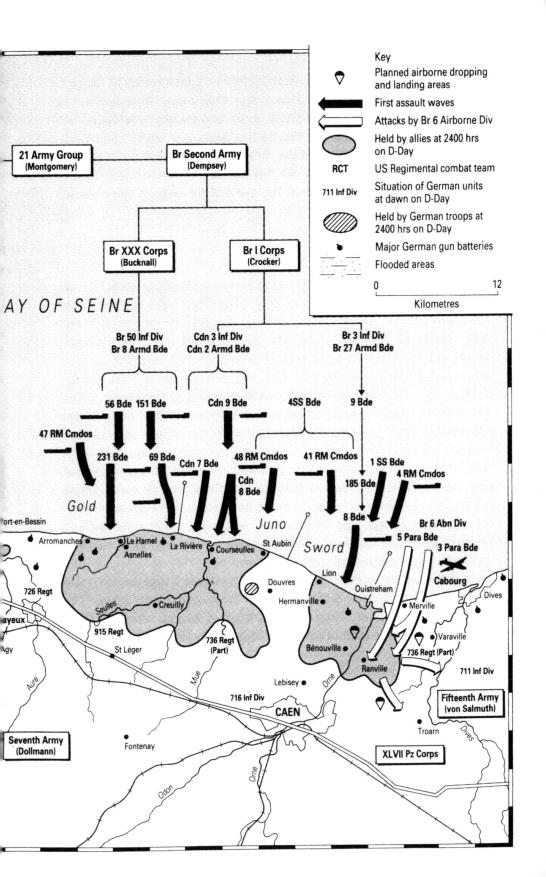

OMAHA BEACH

If the American landing at Utah was achieved with unexpected ease, at Omaha they very nearly came to grief. Here they faced more difficult conditions since a coastal plateau allowed the defenders an unrestricted view across the beaches below. The men boarded their landing craft eleven miles offshore in open seas. This meant that even before they reached the beaches the heavy seas had already taken their toll as landing craft and amphibious tanks were swamped and capsized. When the main landing force came ashore at 6.30 a.m., they found what remained of their vanguard still pinned down at the water's edge and the beaches ahead uncleared. The Americans had opted to use their own bulldozers in preference to British flail tanks to clear their beaches but these, like their engineers, had failed to make it ashore. Ahead of them, holding an advantageous position along the plateau, the German defenders were able to rake the beaches with withering small-arms fire and prevent the Americans from moving forward to clear any of the narrow exits which led from the beaches to the rear.

As the invaders remained stranded at the water's edge or struggled forward in a desperate search for cover, they were mown down. The scene was one of utter chaos with the beaches littered with the debris of wrecked landing craft, equipment and the bodies of the dead and wounded.

Aware of the critical situation, US and British destroyers risked coming close in shore to engage the enemy positions. As the pressure eased, some brave men struggled forward to try and blast a way through one of the beach exits. By 7.30 a.m., the position had started to improve within two hours the Americans were on the plateau and beginning to advance inland towards Vierville-sur-Mer and St Laurent-sur-Mer. By midnight, some thirty-three thousand men were ashore but the three casualties of 'Bloody Omaha' made it the most costly of any of the D-Day landings. On 8 June, the Americans linked up with the British 50th Infantry Division at Port-en-Bessin and joined with their comrades on Utah on 12 June when the two American bridgeheads became one.

GOLD BEACH

Gold Beach, which lay between Le Hamel and La Rivière, was the target of the British 50th Division. After a two-hour-long naval bombardment, the first men ashore at 7.25 a.m. were from the Hampshires, Dorsets, Green Howards and East Yorkshires. At Le Hamel, the Germans held out until mid-day but further to the east the opposition was lighter. Once off the beaches, there was street fighting in St Côme-de-Fresné, Asnelles, Meuvaines and Mont Fleury before troops were able to move inland towards their intended objective, Bayeux. By the evening, troops had entered the outskirts of the town. The 47th Royal Marine Commando advanced westward towards Arromanches-les-Bains and Port-en-Bessin where they finally linked up with the Americans at Omaha on 8 June.

JUNO BEACH

It was Major General R.F.L. Keller's Canadian 3rd Infantry Division that landed on Juno Beach at 7.45 a.m. on D-Day. After prolonged bombing and a naval bombardment, the Royal Winnipeg Rifles, Regina Rifle Regiment, Queen's Own Rifles of Canada and North Shore (New Brunswick) Regiment were the first to land along a stretch of beach which extended from La Rivière across the estuary of the River Seulles to just beyond Langrune-sur-Mer. The landing proved difficult since the beach was protected by a high wall generously dotted with gun emplacements and, like the Americans at Omaha, many of their landing craft floundered in the rough sea so that the first waves of men came ashore ahead of their beach-clearing tanks. However, instead of remaining at the water's edge, they made a dash for it through a hail of small-arms fire to reach the sanctuary of the seafront. Some saw the landing at Juno as a chance to avenge their disaster at Dieppe two years earlier. If this was the case, they certainly succeeded. Of all the Allied divisions, they made the greatest gains on D-Day and, in spite of having to overcome stout German resistance at Courselles-sur-Mer, St Aubin sur Mer and Bernières-sur-Mer, by evening they had managed to advance over sixteen kilometres inland and reached the Caen-Bayeux road at Bretteville-l'Orgueilleuse, close to the airport at Carpiquet.

SWORD BEACH

Sword Beach, at the eastern end of Normandy operations, was the landing area allocated to the British 3rd Infantry Division under Major General T. G. Rennie. It covered the area between Luc-sur-Mer and the estuary of the River Orne at Ouistreham. Here, 'Hobart's Funnies' did successfully make it ashore to clear the beaches and, supported by the tanks of the 13th/18th Hussars, the South Lancashires and East Yorkshires, stormed their way through the seafront defences. Fourth Commando was then able to advance inland to liberate the town of Ouistreham while 41st Royal Marine Commando moved westward to link up with the Canadians at Langrune-sur-Mer.

It was here too that Lord Loval's 1st Special Service Brigade landed to fight its way inland along the Caen Canal to join up with the paratroopers holding Pegasus Bridge. This force included Commandant Kieffer's French Commandos, who were part of No. 10 Inter-Allied Commando.

GREAT ASSAULT GOING WELL

ALLIES SEVERAL MILES INLAND

MASS ATTACK BY AIRBORNE TROOPS

FIGHTING IN CAEN

The Allied Expeditionary Army was fighting last night several miles inland from the beaches of Normandy where it had landed in the morning after the greatest operation of its kind in history.

Mr. Churchill announced last evening that the sea passage had been made " with far less loss than had been apprehended " and the operation was proceeding " in a thoroughly satisfactory manner." Mass airborne landings have been made behind the enemy lines, and the Germans report landings in Guernsey and Jersey.

Upwards of 4,000 ships, together with several thousand smaller craft, are engaged in the operations, and during Monday night more than 5,000 tons of bombs were dropped on ten enemy coastal batteries.

WAITING FOR THE WORD

A VAST GATHERING

FINAL MOVES TO THE SEA

From Our Special Correspondent

AN ENGLISH PORT, JUNE 5

The time has come. All we await now is the word to go forth and strike the terrific blow in Western Europe, of which General Montgomery writes in his valediction to the assault troops under his command. When this despatch appears that blow will have been struck ; and as one gazes out over an anchorage of fond remembrance in which, framed by the sweep of England's green shore, countless invasion ships lie at their stations, the mind recoils from the dimensions of it all.

For these tight-packed ships represent only one of the rivers of men and machines that all along the coast are pouring out into the sea. Four years ago, almost to the day, the tide of war had flooded from the east into the French channel ports before swirling back on Paris and far beyond. Now the tide has turned, and in this suspended moment of history the first mighty wave is gathered before it crashes down on the enemy's beaches. And the near observer gets no more than the fleeting, awesome glimpse of it that a solitary swimmer would have of a great breaker in an angry sea.

The mightiest armada of all time—such phrases come glibly but say very little. Words, indeed, pale before the vastness of the reality ; and writing aboard an American landing craft, a veteran of Sicily, Salerno, and Anzio—a happy omen, this—I can attempt no more than to sketch in some of the impressions that have crowded upon us during the embarcation period.

D-day report in *The Times* on 7 June 1944.

In spite of these early successes, the progress of the units which landed at Sword proved disappointing. Inland, they ran into stiff German resistance between Douvres-la-Délivrande and Bénouville and made little further progress. The German strongpoint 'Hillman' above Colleville-sur-Mer (now Colleville-Montgomery) proved particularly difficult to overcome and contributed to the loss of momentum. The delay meant that any realistic hope of reaching Caen rapidly faded and, although the 2nd King's Own Shropshire Light Infantry did reach a point only six kilometres short, there was to be a further period of six weeks' bitter fighting before the city fell.

DER WASSERSCHEUE KLEINE WINSTON

A German cartoon of early 1944 portrays Winston Churchill as a child who is scared of the water. Stalin had long urged the Allies to open a Second Front in the West and here the Russian leader is shown pushing an unwilling Britain towards the prospect of an 'Invasion'.

The overall result of the D-Day operations was that the Allies had breached Hitler's 'Atlantic Wall' and won themselves a foothold on the continent of Europe. In spite of adverse weather conditions and variable German resistance, something over 132,000 men (75,000 British and Canadians and 57,000 Americans) with their equipment and vehicles had been landed along the Normandy coast. It was a magnificent achievement but, even so, it was to be three weeks before the Americans took Cherbourg (27 June), six weeks before the British and Canadians took Caen (10 July) and nearly three months before Allied troops liberated Paris (25 August).

The cost was far less than had been feared. The total casualties were some 10,200 and of these 4,200 were British and Canadian and 6,000 American – half of them on Omaha. The number of Allied killed was no more than 2,500, small perhaps if compared with the 19,240 who died on the first day of the Battle of the Somme in 1916. On the evening of the 6 June 1944, Winston Churchill addressed the House of Commons:

Many dangers and difficulties hich at this time last night appeared to e extremely formidable are behind us. The passage of the sea has been made with far less loss than we

Left: Stephen Roth's cartoon of 1943, *'The Sword of Damocles'*, shows Hitler cringing in bed as Churchill counts down towards the opening of a Second Front.
Right: A *Punch* cartoon carries virtually the same message. In *'No Cure for Insomnia'*, Hitler lies awake anticipating the storming of his Atlantic Wall.

apprehended. The resistance of the batteries has been greatly weakened by the bombing of our Air Force, and the superior bombardment of our ships quickly reduced their fire dimensions which did nt affect the problem. The landings of the troops on a broad front, both British and American, have been effective, and our troops have penetrated, in some cases, several miles inland. Lodgments exist on a broad front ... But all this, although a very valuable first step – a vital and essential first step – gives no indication of what may be the course of the battle in the next few days and weeks ... It is, therefore, a most serious time we enter upon. Thank God, we enter upon it with our great Allies all in good heart and all in good friendship.

On D-Day plus six, it was possible for the British prime minister to cross to France, on whose soil he had last stood in the bleak days of June 1940 when the country was at the point of surrendering to the Nazi invaders.

7 June 1944. In the *Daily Mirror* Zec shows Allied troops storming Hitler's European fortress. A British soldier clutches a 'Bill' – the score for a catalogue of crimes now to be settled.

Illingworth of the *Daily Mail* warns Hitler that *'This is it!'*

6

WAR POETS OF THE NORMANDY CAMPAIGN

The Great War, 1914-18, produced a number of poets whose works have achieved worldwide recognition – Brooke, McCrae, Owen, Rosenberg and Sassoon. Extracts from their poems are known to every schoolboy – 'If I should die, think only this of me ...', 'In Flanders fields the poppies grow ...', 'What passing bells for those who die as cattle?', 'Dulce et decorum est pro patria mori'. Second World War poets have failed to achieve such prominence. Is it that their message is less strong, their style less emotive? I think not. The fact is that the Second World War has failed to stir the type of pathos generated by the First. Nostalgia for the years 1939 to 1945 abounds, as is evident in the popularity of the numerous films and television series about the Second World War. The music of that war largely retains its popularity but not its poetry.

The Second World War produced more poets than the Great War and their works are often as powerful as those of the bards of the trenches but they do not dwell on patriotism nor represent the dire and sanguine consequences of a static war of attrition. They have yet to become vogue, they have yet to be considered worthy of inclusion in schools' English literature curricula. Maybe the passing of the years will achieve this.

The poems that follow are but a token selection from the vast amount available and the poets have one thing in common -they were all involved, in one way or another, in the Normandy campaign.

Alexander McKee OBE, FRGS, writer and producer of radio documentaries, is the man who located the wreck of Henry VIII's warship, the *Mary Rose*. During the Second World War, he served with the London Scottish and the Gordon Highlanders. He landed in Normandy in July 1944 and was attached to the Headquarters of the Canadian 1st Army.

Maple leaf down

Normandy, focus of the world in summer,
All eyes, all thoughts upon you,
And a million men locked up in Calvados.

Your roads like deserts, deep in dust,
Dust that cloaked the fields and the blue
And rose-entwined meandering
Of trellis-work upon your cottages of stone.
A summer blue with skies, in Normandy,
And white with cumulus and dust,
And black with smoke of battle.
Like serpents, the armies crawled up from the sea,
And writhed upon your roads;
A vast armada lay, two-score mile of ships,
About your burning beaches, and the spires
Of Courseulles and Arromanches
Were but prelude to the guns of Caen,
Of Villers Bocage, and the heights before Falaise.

All that is gone, down corridors of memory
I see the bullet-marks on white-clad walls,
And stone churches standing in the hills,
The windings of the Seulles and of the Orne,
The perfumed blue of Norman night,
And the stars, ragged in the trees.

All that is gone: buried at the end of all the years,
Beneath the weight of other memory.
But if I go back so far in time
That the Rhineland plain shall fade,
And the jagged towers of Arnhem,
The bleak and wintry Maas, and Antwerp
In her vale of pain; and stride down the years –
Past Ghent in autumn, and Calais
Standing at the last gate of summer,
By Abbeville and Beauvais, across the Seine,
I shall come at last to you again. Again
You shall be mistress of my dreams,
The end, as once you were the beginning,
The gateway to Europe, of the path that leads us home.

ALEXANDER McKEE

Melville Hardiment was a regular soldier with the East Yorks Regiment. A sergeant, he landed in Normandy on D-Day and was later wounded at Touffreville during the battle for Caen.

Poor dead Panzer

Poor dead Panzer!
It must have cost you some
to crawl through this wheat
setting it alight,
into this ditch
where swollen flies
buzz round the stiff upturned legs
of a Uccello cart-horse:
And you must have hated the stench
of what you now stink too.
Dragging your torn shoulder
through the corn, an oily smudge
on your tunic sizzling, and clutching
to your chest this evil looking
Schmeisser machine pistol I covet,
and which sure you must have treasured
to spin round it a frothy cocoon
of brain tissues and dried blood
oozing from that hole in your forehead?

Poor old Panzer!
You sought to protect it so,
did you not? And you felt less vulnerable
with it in your hand.
Now here I am – half Jew
the victorious invader –
dispossessing you.

And as I take the butt
into my plough-hands
seeking the point of balance,
I catch a whiff of Bavarian
harvest fields and temporarily
drop it back beside you.

MELVILLE HARDIMENT

François Édouard Macé was born in London of Anglo-French parents. In 1939 at the outbreak of war he enlisted in the Rifle Brigade. Promoted to lance corporal, he landed in Normandy in June 1944 and served with the 11th Armoured Division. The padre mentioned in the poem has been identified as the Reverend H. J. Taylor, who was awarded the Military Cross for saving the lives of two wounded men during the height of battle.

The padre

Greenjackets
Eleventh Armoured Division
Charging black bull, badge of Mithras
Bridgehead breakout, Orne and Odon
Hill 112
Out of the battle for a refit
In a field at Bretteville l'Orgueilleuse
Service in a few minutes, Communion after
Disperse on air attack.

Coming, brother?
Me? In Civvy Street I'm a dustman
Quipped the sergeant – childhood echo –
Jesus wants you for a sunbeam
Clouds they parted and a voice said:
In no wise will I cast him out.

Unwashed, unshaven
All hands soiled, including padre's
Oil and petrol
Blood, earth and sweat, et cet
Surplice dirty, torn and crumpled
Sleepless eyes and slurring speech
Military Cross and death hid future
Pulpit bonnet, altar bumper
Wine long finished
Wafers halved, then quartered, crumbled ...
Carry on to the Amen.

Time and water – wash and shave
Take a pickaxe and a spade

Unto God's most gracious mercy
Go bury now your youthful dead.

F. E. MACÉ

A Welshman, John Ottewell, the scriptwriter and broadcaster, was born at Brecon. In 1943, he joined the Royal Welch Fusiliers and went to Normandy in June 1944.

'Evrecy', July 1944

Men of the 'Black Flash', 'Sospan' and 'Dragon',
Wading through 'Bayonet' wheat, knee-high and wet,
Mortars and 'eighty-eights' playing their 'overtures'
Spandaus and Schmeissers are waiting and 'set' ...

Up to the hill enshrouded in mortar smoke,
Tellermines, 'S' mines, a'mushroom the slope,
'Tiger' tanks, 'panzerfausts' blasting our 'carriers' ...
'Air burst' exploding like 'bubbles of soap'...

Now across the singing Guighe into the alder wood,
Remnants of companies merged to platoon.
Screams for the stretchers with 'Mother' and 'Jesus!!',
'Steady old son ... we'll have you out soon'!!

Men of the 'Black Flash', 'Sospan' and 'Dragon'
Limping it back ... all haggard and pale,
Two hundred dead for a handful of prisoners,
Just one consolation ... 'They've brought up the Mail'!!

JOHN A. OTTEWELL

A captain in the 51st Highland Division, John Jarmain had earlier served in the Western Desert. He landed in Normandy after D-Day and was killed in action at St Honorine la Chardonnerette on 26 June 1944. He had a premonition of his impending death and was killed by a mortar bomb while on a recce patrol.

At a war grave

No grave is rich, the dust that herein lies
Beneath this white cross mixing with the sand
Was vital once, with skill of eye and hand
And speed of brain. These will not re-arise
These riches, nor will they be replaced:
They are lost and nothing now, and here is left
Only a worthless corpse of sense bereft,
Symbol of death, and sacrifice and waste.

JOHN J. ARMAIN

The SHAEF team. *From l. to r.:* Lieutenant General Omar Bradley, Admiral Sir Bertram Ramsay, Air Chief Marshal Sir Arthur Tedder, General Dwight D. Eisenhower, General Sir Bernard Montgomery, Air Marshal Sir Trafford Leigh-Mallory and Lieutenant General Walter Bedell Smith.

Left: Field Marshal Erwin Rommel, who commanded German Army Group B in France

Right: Field Marshal Gerd von Rundstedt, German Commander-in-Chief in Normandy

Field Marshal Rommel with his entourage inspecting coastal defences in Normandy. The poles with mines attached were submerged at high tide and were expected to take a great toll of the landing craft of any invasion fleet.

Today a great deal of Hitler's much vaunted Atlantic Wall is still to be found along the French coastline. Remains of emplacements at Longues-sur-Mer.

Sherman tanks stock-piled in readiness in Dorset.

A completed section of a Mulberry harbour waiting to be towed to the assembly points along the south coast.

Wrecked gliders close to the Caen canal bridge. To the left is the café run by the Gondrée family.

British troops crossing Pegasus Bridge. The gliders can be seen to the right among the trees. The close proximity of the gliders to the bridge gives some idea of the skill of the glider pilots that night.

Left: Major General Richard Gale, who commanded the British 6th Airborne Division.

Right: Major John Howard, who led the glider-borne troops that captured Pegasus Bridge on the morning of 6 June.

An American paratrooper rests near a signpost on the outskirts of Ste Mère-Église. An American paratrooper rests near a signpost on the outskirts of Ste Mère-Église.

Left: An American solider watches for German snipers in the church tower in the square at Ste Mère-Église.

Below: Against a menacing background, with the beach already littered with bodies, American soldiers wade ashore at 'bloody' Omaha.

Right: American Rangers making their way to the top of the Pointe du Hoc.

Below: Colonel Rudder's command post marked with the US flag. A group of German prisoners is led away.

An aerial photograph shows the extent of the Allied bombing of the gun positions of the Merville Battery before D-Day.

Left: Leutnant Raimund Steiner, the German officer who commanded the Merville Battery.
Right: Major John Pooley, who led the British No. 3 Commando during the assault on the battery.

7

VICTORIA CROSSES AWARDED DURING THE NORMANDY CAMPAIGN

🐾 CSM STANLEY HOLLIS

Middlesbrough-born CSM Hollis of the 6th Battalion, The Green Howards, was the only man to be awarded the Victoria Cross for acts of bravery on 6 June 1944. CSM Hollis's unit went ashore on Gold Beach. After his company had moved inland, he returned with his company commander to investigate two German pillboxes which had been by-passed at Mont Fleury. He rushed forward towards the first and killed all but five of the occupants and these were taken prisoner. He then dealt with the second and succeeded in capturing a further twenty-six prisoners. During the rest of the day, he was always to be found in the thick of the fighting and it was largely due to his heroism that his company achieved their objectives and that their casualties were not heavier. After the war he returned to Middlesbrough where he died in 1972 aged fifty-nine.

🐾 CORPORAL SIDNEY BATES

Twenty-three-year-old Corporal Bates served in The Royal Norfolk Regiment and came from Camberwell in London's East End. It was on 6 August 1944 at Sourdeval to the south of Vire that the corporal realised that German troops had penetrated the area around his section. He immediately seized a light machine-gun and charged forward through a hail of bullets. Although twice wounded, he remained undaunted and continued firing until the enemy began to withdraw. At this moment, he was wounded for the third time but still continued to engage the enemy until his strength failed him. By this time, the Germans had retreated and his section's situation was secure. Two days later Corporal Bates died from his wounds and today his grave is to be found in Bayeux War Cemetery.

CAPTAIN DAVID JAMIESON

Captain Jamieson, who came from Thornham, King's Lynn, served in the same regiment as Corporal Bates and earned his Victoria Cross on the following day. On 7/8 August 1944, a company under the captain's command managed to secure a bridgehead over the River Orne just to the south of Grimbosq. During the next thirty-six hours, when the fighting was savage and hand-to-hand, the company withstood seven German counter-attacks. There were times when the situation seemed near hopeless but, inspired by Captain Jamieson's leadership and personal bravery, his men managed to hold on to the bridgehead. Although twice wounded, the officer steadfastly refused to be evacuated. After the war, he served as one of HM Body Guard, Honourable Corps of Gentlemen-at-Arms and, in 1980, was appointed High Sheriff of Norfolk.

LIEUTENANT TASKER WATKINS

Twenty-six years old and from Nelson in Glamorgan, Lieutenant Tasker Watkins served in the l/5th Battalion of The Welch Regiment. On 16 August 1944 at Barfour, Lieutenant Watkins's company came under murderous machine-gun fire while advancing through corn fields set with booby traps. The sole surviving officer and with only thirty men left, he led a bayonet charge against a superior force of Germans and virtually wiped them out. At nightfall and with his company cut off from the rest of the battalion, he ordered his men to disperse. Then, when he had personally charged and silenced a machine-gun position, he led them back to safety. His leadership not only saved his men but also decisively influenced the outcome of the battle. After the war, the Rt. Hon. Lord Justice Watkins, as he became, was an eminent member of the legal profession and served as Judge (1974), a Lord Justice of Appeal (1980), Senior Presiding Judge for England and Wales (1983), Deputy Chief Justice of England (1988) and the President of the Welsh Rugby Union.

MAJOR DAVID CURRIE

From Sutherland, Saskatchewan, Major David Currie served in the 29th Canadian Armoured Reconnaissance Regiment (The South Alberta Regiment). During the period 18-20 August 1944, at the Battle of Falaise, Major Currie was in command of a force sent to cut one of the remaining German escape routes out of the 'Falaise pocket'. His unit fought its way into the village of St Lambert-sur-Dives and there established a defensive position. For thirty-six hours they held their ground against repeated enemy attacks. Altogether they destroyed seven enemy tanks and forty other vehicles. In addition, three hundred Germans were killed, five hundred wounded and 1,100 taken prisoner. Although the Canadians suffered heavy casualties, Major Currie's inspired leadership denied the Germans use of this escape route. After the war, Lieutenant Colonel Currie served as the Seargeant-at-Arms of the House of Commons in Ottawa. He died in 1986.

8

VISITING THE CEMETERIES OF THE COMMONWEALTH WAR GRAVES COMMISSION

Something approaching 1,700,000 Commonwealth sailors, soldiers and airmen were killed in the two World Wars. Today the majority of these men lie buried in cemeteries maintained by the Commonwealth War Graves Commission which are to be found worldwide in some 140 different countries. In France alone there are 2,940 burial grounds containing over 465,00 Commonwealth graves and, in Belgium, a further 628 burial grounds with some 149,000 graves. The vast majority of these date from the Great War, 1914-18.

As a consequence of the Second World War, 1939–45, the Commission tends over 50,000 graves in the Far East, 46,000 in Italy, 45,000 in North Africa, 32,000 in Germany, 19,000 in the Netherlands and 15,000 in Greece. In addition, the Commission's memorials commemorate the 232,990 missing servicemen of the Second World War as well as 6,373 civilians whose deaths were due to enemy action.

In the Calvados region of Normandy there are eighteen Commonwealth War Cemeteries containing the graves of 22,410 men who lost their lives on D-Day. 6 June 1944, and during the weeks that followed. Some servicemen also lie in civilian cemeteries or are to be found in individual plots in numerous churchyards across the region. A further 1,808 men who have no known graves are commemorated by name on the panels of the Bayeux War Memorial which is situated opposite the Bayeux War Cemetery, the largest of the Second World War cemeteries to be found in France.

Founded by Royal Charter in 1917, the Imperial War Graves Commission, as it was originally known, set out to remember the sacrifice of each of the fallen, either by a permanent grave or, where the serviceman is missing and has no known resting place, by an inscription on a memorial. Visitors to the Commission's cemeteries are ever empressed by the standards of maintenance and by the care shown by their gardening staff. The land on which the cemeteries stand has been given as a free gift by the French people 'for the perpetual resting place of the sailors, and soldiers and airmen who are honoured here'. Irrespective of size or location, each cemetery has an atmosphere of reverence and tranquillity.

At each cemetery, a register can be found in a bronze locker which is set into the wall near the entrance or situated in the shelter. The register gives details of those buried there and of the location of each grave. The locker also contains a visitors' book. The cemeteries are landscaped, with the graves set in rows to stand in narrow borders of flowers and shrubs. The curved headstones are of a standard pattern and made from stone taken from the Portland or Hopton Wood Quarries. Each carries details of the serviceman's name, rank, number and decorations, together with his regimental or corps badge. Each also bears an appropriate religious symbol. The headstones of Commonwealth servicemen carry the national emblem of their homelands. Holders of the Victoria Cross have the distinctive Maltese cross with the inscription 'For Valour' engraved on their headstones. Graves of those who could not be identified carry an inscription chosen originally by Rudyard Kipling, then literary advisor to the Commission, 'A Soldier of the Second World War Known unto God'.

Most cemeteries include a Cross of Sacrifice and, in all but the smallest, a Stone of Remembrance. The Cross of Sacrifice was designed by Sir Reginald Blomfield RA and the altar-like Stone of Remembrance by Sir Edwin Lutyens RA. Its inscription, 'Their Nanle Liveth for Evermore', was suggested by Kipling and taken from the Apocrypha. Chapter 44 of Ecclesiasticus, which begins 'Let us now praise famous men, and our fathers that begat us', continues in verse 14, 'Their bodies are buried in peace; but their name liveth for evermore'.

A visitor searching for a particular grave should first contact the headquarters of the Commonwealth War Graves Commission to discover the place of burial. At the cemetery, the register includes a plan and details of the plot, row and number of each grave. A casual search of a large cemetery can be very time-consuming and, possibly, unrewarding. The Commission has published a booklet, *Normandy June-August 1944: Guide to the Commonwealth War Cemeteries and the Bayeux Memorial*, and also has available for sale copies of cemetery and memorial registers. It will usually provide a photocopy of an individual page from the registers. Although the Commission does not operate an official photographic service, it will attempt to provide photographs of individual graves, cemeteries and memorials. The headquarters of the Commonwealth War Graves Commission are at:

2 Marlow Road, Maidenhead
Berkshire SL6 7DX
(Tel: 01628–34221)

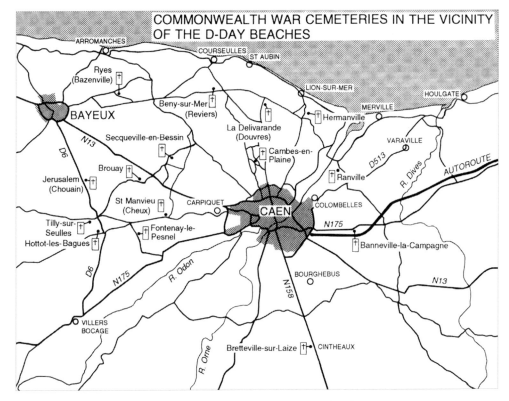

Map of commonwealth war cemeteries in the vicinity of the D-Day beaches.

COMMONWEALTH WAR CEMETERIES IN NORMANDY
(with number of burials)

✝ Banneville-la-Campagne   2,175
✝ Bayeux   4,648
✝ Bény-sur-Mer (Reviers)   2,049
✝ Bretteville-sur-Laize   2,958
✝ Brouay   377
✝ Cambes-en-Plaine   224
✝ La Délivrande (Douvres)   1,123
✝ Fontenay-le-Pesnel   520
✝ Hermanville   1,005
✝ Hottot-les-Bagues   1,137
✝ Jerusalem (Chouain)   47
✝ Ranville   2,562

✝ Ryes (Bazenville)   979
✝ St Charles de Percy   789
✝ St Désir   598
✝ St Manvieu (Cheux)   2,183
✝ Secqueville-en-Bessin   117
✝ Tilly-sur-Seulles   1,222)

OTHER GRAVES OF BRITISH AND COMMONWEALTH SERVICEMEN IN NORMANDY

A number of Norman churchyards and town cemeteries contain the graves of British servicemen of the Second World War. In some instances they were RAF personnel whose aircraft were brought down in the area; in others, they were soldiers killed on D-Day or soon afterwards whose bodies were buried locally and have remained there. There are a few graves of men of the BEF who lost their lives in 1940 and some of men who fell during the Great War, 1914-18.

✝ Basly churchyard   1
✝ Bavent churchyard   1
✝ Bénouville churchyard   23
✝ Biéville-en-Auge churchyard   1
✝ Biéville-sur-Orne churchyard   5
✝ Blonville-sur-Mer churchyard   1
✝ Bonnebosq churchyard   2
✝ Branville churchyard   1
✝ Bretteville-sur-Dives churchyard   1
✝ Bréville communal cemetery   2
✝ Brucourt churchyard   6
✝ Cabourg communal cemetery   1
✝ Cagny communal cemetery   6
✝ Cahagnes (at roadside)   1
✝ Cambremer communal cemetery   1
✝ Castillon-en-Auge churchyard   1
✝ Caumont L'Éventé communal cemetery   1
✝ Chênedollé churchyard   1
✝ Clarbec churchyard   1
✝ Colleville-sur-Mer churchyard   1
✝ Coulvain churchyard   7
✝ Crépon churchyard   2

✝ Crèvecoeur-en-Auge communal cemetery	1
✝ Cricqueville-en-Auge churchyard	1
✝ Culey-le-Patry communal cemetery	1
✝ Dives-sur-Mer communal cemetery	1
✝ Écots churchyard	1
✝ Ellon churchyard	2
✝ Escoville churchyard	1
✝ Espins churchyard	1
✝ Fervaques (behind church)	1
✝ Fierville les Parcs churchyard	1
✝ Frénouville churchyard	1
✝ Gavrus churchyard	1
✝ Grandcamp-Maisy communal cemetery	1
✝ Hérouvillette new communal cemetery	27
✝ Honfleur (St Léonard) communal cemetery	7
✝ Houlgate (Beuzeval) communal cemetery	10
✝ Juaye-Mondaye communal cemetery	1
✝ La Bigne churchyard	1
✝ La Boissière churchyard	1
✝ La Chappelle-Yvon churchyard	1
✝ La Cressonnière churchyard	1
✝ Le Mesnil-Durand communal cemetery	1
✝ Le Pré-d'Auge churchyard	1
✝ Les Loges-Saulces churchyard	4
✝ Les Moutiers-Hubert churchyard	4
✝ Le Torquesne churchyard	1
✝ Lisieux communal cemetery	12
✝ Livry churchyard	3
✝ Luc-sur-Mer churchyard	3
✝ Magny churchyard	1
✝ Marolles churchyard	1
✝ Merville-Franceville-Plage churchyard	7
✝ Missy churchyard	1
✝ Mouen churchyard	1
✝ Noyers-Bocage churchyard	2
✝ Osmanville (St Clément) churchyard	1
✝ Ouistreham-Riva Bella communal cemetery	5
✝ Percy-en-Auge churchyard	1
✝ Périers-en-Auge churchyard	1

✟ Pont-l'Évêque (Route de Caen) communal   4
  cemetery
✟ Putot-en-Auge churchyard   32
✟ Quetteville churchyard   1)
✟ Quetteville communal cemetery   2
✟ Rocques churchyard   1
✟ St Crespin churchyard   3
✟ Ste Honorine-des-Pertes churchyard   1
✟ St Hymer churchyard   1
✟ St Lambert churchyard   1
✟ St Laurent-sur-Mer churchyard   3
✟ St Loup-de-Fribois churchyard   2
✟ Ste Marguerite-des-Loges churchyard   2
✟ St Martin-de-Sallen communal cemetery   2
✟ St Martin-des-Entrées (St Germain) cemetery   1
✟ St Remy churchyard   2
✟ St Samson churchyard   1
✟ St Sever-Calvados communal cemetery   6
✟ St Vaast-en-Auge churchyard   12
✟ Sassy churchyard   1
✟ Sully churchyard   1
✟ Touffreville churchyard   1
✟ Tourgéville military cemetery (a Great War   13
  cemetery with Second World War British and
  Commonwealth burials)
✟ Tourville-sur-Odon churchyard   6
✟ Troarn communal cemetery   3
✟ Trouville communal cemetery   4
✟ Ussy churchyard   1
✟ Vaudry churchyard   1
✟ Vauville churchyard   1
✟ Villerville communal cemetery   2
✟ Villers-le-Sec churchyard   2
✟ Vire new communal cemetery   4

9

D-DAY AND NORMANDY CAMPAIGN MUSEUMS

The following museums are generally open all the year round, though opening times may be variable. Each has a comprehensive collection of artefacts, documents and photographs and many show archival/documentary films or have audio-visual presentations. The Memorial Museum at Caen holds extensive collections and is particularly impressive. Each museum makes an admission charge.

ARROMANCHES

MUSÉE DU DÉBARQUEMENT
Rue du Marechal Joffre
Arromanches
Tel: 31 21 47 56
Daily except for the first three weeks in January

BAYEUX

MUSÉE MEMORIAL DE LA BATAILLE DE NORMANDIE
Boulevard Fabian Ware
Bayeux
Tel: 31 92 93 41
Daily

BÉNOUVILLE (PEGASUS BRIDGE)

MUSÉE DES TROUPES AÉROPORTÉES
Avenue du Commandant Kieffer

Bénouville
Tel: 31 44 62 54
Daily

CAEN

MEMORIAL – UN MUSÉE POUR LA PAIX
Place du General Eisenhower
Caen
Tel: 31 06 06 44
Daily except for first two weeks in January

CHERBOURG

MUSÉE DE LA GUERRE ET DE LA LIBÉRATION
Fort du Roule
Cherbourg
Tel: 33 20 14 12
Daily except Tuesdays

SAINT MARIE DU MONT

MUSÉE DE DÉBARQUEMENT
Plage de la Madeline
Saint Marie du Mont
Tel: 33 71 53 35
Daily except in January

SAINTE MÈRE-ÉGLISE

AIRBORNE MUSEUM
Place du 6 Juin 1944
Ste Mère-Église
Tel: 33 41 41 35
Daily except 16 December to 31 January

Other museums are usually only open for part of the year and their displays, though interesting, are often more limited. These include:

COLLEVILLE-MONTGOMERY

MUSEUM 6 JUIN 1944
in the town on the D514
Variable. Need to check in advance

HERMANVILLE-SUR-MER

SWORD BEACH EXHIBITION
La Brèche
June to August and some weekends

MERVILLE-FRANCEVILLE

MERVILLE BATTERY MUSEUM
Avenue de la Batterie de Merville
Merville-Franceville
Tel: 31 24 21 83
June, July and August but not Tuesdays

OUISTREHAM-RIVA BELLA

No.4 COMMANDO MUSEUM
Place Alfred Thomas
Ouistreham-Riva Bella
Tel: 31 96 63 10
May to mid-September

ATLANTIC WALL MUSEUM
Avenue du 6 Juin
Ouistreham-Riva Bella
Tel: 31 97 28 69
Daily

SURRAIN

MUSÉE DE LA LIBÉRATION DE NORMANDIE
Off the N 13
Daily

TILLY-SUR-SEULLES

MUSÉE DE LA BATAILLE DE TILLY-SUR-SEULLES
Rue du 18 Juin 1944
Chapelle Notre Dame-du-Val
Tilly-sur-Seulles
Tel: 31 8083 11
June, July and August and weekends in September

VIERVILLE-SUR-MER

EXPOSITION OMAHA
Off the DS14 on leaving the town
April to September

Opposite: A detail from an RAC road map of the area of the Normandy landings.

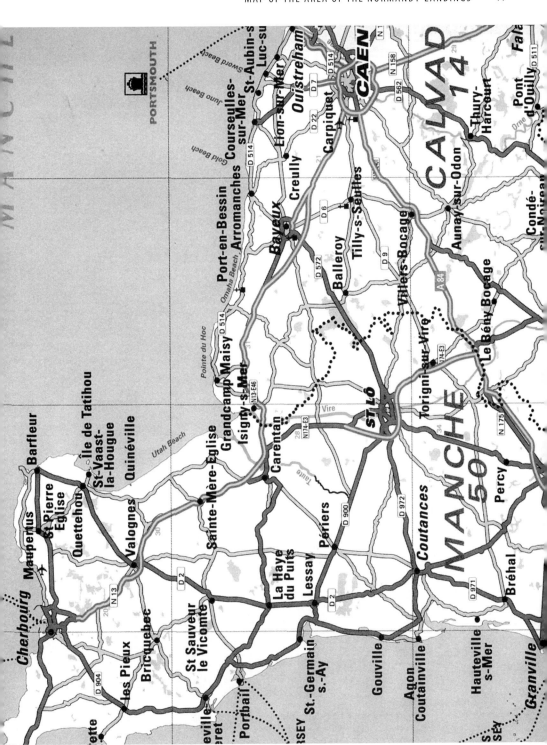

GAZETTEER

🐃 AMFREVILLE

Amfreville, which is twinned with Dolton in Devon, lies on the eastern bank of the River Orne. After crossing Pegasus Bridge, the village can be reached by travelling towards Sallenelles on the D514 for about five kilometres. It is signposted and lies on the right hand side.

The village, which is scattered around a green with a church in the centre, was liberated by the men of No. 6 Commando on the morning of D-Day and afterwards was part of an extended salient which protected the eastern flank of the British positions. It became the scene of prolonged, heavy fighting which involved the 12th Parachute Battalion and the Devonshires. The green, 'Le Plain Place du Commandant Kieffer', was named after Captain Philippe Kieffer, leader of the French No. 7 and No. 8 Troops which were part of No.4 Commando. Close to the church are No.6 Commando Memorial, a memorial to Lord Lovat's First Special Service Brigade, and a memorial to the British and French Commandos who 'landed from the sea on the morning of D-Day, 6th June 1944, and fought their way inland to join the 6th Airborne Division. Together they held the eastern flank secure against all enemy attacks throughout· the Normandy campaign'. Follow the D37b to the edge of the village and tum along the Rue Oger, to reach the memorial to No. 4 Commando – the Hoger No.4 Commando Memorial – so-called because at the time British soldiers tended to pronounce Oger as 'Hoger'.

🐃 ARROMANCHES

Arromanches-les-Bains is one of the· most popular resorts along the Normandy coast and, because of its association with D-Day and Port Winston, the artificial harbour, it attracts a great many British tourists each year. The town can be approached directly from Bayeux along the D516 or from both east and west by following the D514 coast road. At peak holiday times, the centre of the town is very busy and parking can be difficult. In June 1944, Arromanches-les-Bains was a small seaside resort important to the Germans because of its strategically-based radar station. A week before D-Day, these installations were destroyed by Allied air attacks.

On D-Day, Arromanches lay just outside the extreme western edge of the designated landing area within Gold Beach -the initial landings took place between Asnelles and La Rivière. Once the 1st Hampshires and 1st Dorsets had cleared the beaches immediately to the east of the town, dogged German resistance at Le Hamel slowed the British advance along the coast towards Arromanches. Reinforced by units of the 7th Armoured Division, they gradually fought their way forward and the first British tanks entered Arromanches at 4 p.m. on the afternoon of D-Day. Stoutly defended by German troops of 352 Division, the town did not completely fall until the next day, when it was finally liberated by men of 47 Royal Marine Commando advancing from St Côme-de-Fresné. Work immediately began on the construction of the artificial harbour, 'Mulberry B', later to be known as Port Winston.

Until such time as a major port, such as Cherbourg or Le Havre, was in Allied hands, it was planned to use two specially constructed prefabricated harbours to land the essential supplies and reinforcements needed by the invasion forces. To make this possible, 'Force Mulberry' had made its way across the Channel behind the main invasion fleet at a laborious four knots. This fleet was made up of 'Gooseberries' (block ships), 'Phoenix' caissons (massive blocks of concrete towed by tugs) and escort ships. It was intended to establish two such prefabricated harbours, 'Mulberry A' off Omaha Beach for use by the Americans and 'Mulberry B' at Arromanches on Gold Beach for the British. Once in osition, the 'Gooseberries' were sunk to provide a breakwater and the ~Phoenixes" each over sixty metres long and some the size of a three-storey building, were placed in position to form an outer sea wall. These were then connected to the land by a system of linked piers and pontoon bridges, capable of moving up and down to accommodate the rise and fall of the Normandy tides. 'Mulberry B' at Arromanches was completed by 10 June and became a vital supply artery for the invasion forces. During the following hundred days, some 2,500,000 men, 54,000 vehicles and 104,000 tonnes of supplies came ashore here -the amount landed each day compared favourably with that of the port of Le Havre before the war!

Between 17 and 22 June, storms raged in the English Channel as north-easterly winds sent large waves smashing against the artificial constructions. At Omaha Beach, the American 'Mulberry A' was damaged beyond repair but at Arromanches the main breakwater held so that the harbour could be quickly restored and made operational again.

Today Arromanches-les-Bains is a bustling resort with numerous hotels and a great many souvenir shops, cafés, bars and restaurants clustered around its busy square and promenade. In the square is the impressive D-Day Museum. This was opened in 1954 by the French President, René Coty, and it contains a unique collection of documents and photographs covering every aspect of the invasion. There are also relief maps, working models, luminous and sound dioramas with French and English commentaries, displays of weapons and a cinema with regular film shows. Just outside are a number of artillery pieces and vehicles including a Sherman tank. The Museum is open all the year round. Out to sea and quite easily visible are the remains of 'Mulberry B'. At low tide, it is possible to reach sections closest to the shore.

Opposite the Office de Tourisme is a memorial to those who flew with the Free French – *the Groupe Lorraine* of the Forces *Aériennes Françaises Libres*. The memorial lists the numerous theatres of war in which the unit served.

🐾 ASNELLES

The coastal village of Asnelles lies just beyond St Côme-de-Fresné on the D514 between Arromanches-les-Bains and Ver-sur-Mer.

On D-Day, it was here and at adjacent Le Hamel that the men of the 231st Infantry Brigade of the 50th Northumbrian Division led the way ashore at H-hour – 7.25 a.m. The Brigade, which included the 1st Dorsets, 2nd Devonshires and 1st Hampshires, was supported by RAF sorties and broadsides from HMS *Ajax* of 'Battle of the River Plate' fame. Even so, the Hampshires came under heavy fire from German machine-guns and mortars and found it difficult to move off the beach. By the end of the day the Battalion's casualties totalled sixteen officers and 166 men. Their wounded included their commanding officer, Lieutenant Colonel Nelson Smith. By the next day they had cleared the area so that they held a perimeter around Le Hamel, Asnelles, Arromanches-les-Bains, Tracy-sur-Mer and Manvieux. It was also along this section of Gold Beach that 'Hobart's Funnies' first made their appearance.

The crossroads in the centre of the village is named after the commander of 231st Infantry Brigade, Place Alexander Stanier, and nearby there is a Rue de Southampton. In the Rue The Devonshire Regiment, there is an unusual, wall-like monument to the 50th Northumbrian Division. It is inscribed, *'A Ses Glorieux Libérateurs – La Commune d'Asnelles le Hamel – Reconnaissante – 6 Juin 1944'*. Close by on the seafront there is a German bunker and from this vantage point it is possible to look westward towards Arromanches-les-Bains and, out to sea, the remains of the Mulberry harbour.

🐾 AUDRIEU

Audrieu is a small village on the D82 just to the west of Brouay. Somewhat out of the way, it is best reached by following the N13 Caen to Bayeux road for twelve kilometres and at Silo turn to the left along the D158 which joins the D82 just before entering the village.

On the 8 June, the positions held by the Royal Winnipeg Rifles to the north-west of Caen were overrun by the. fanatical teenagers of Colonel Kurt Meyer's 12th SS Panzers, which were part of the Hitler *Jugend* Division. There were heavy losses on both sides and many Canadians were taken prisoner. In the village, on the wall opposite the church, is a memorial to the men of the Royal Winnipeg Rifles who were murdered by the Germans while being held as prisoners-of-war. These atrocities occurred on the 8, 9 and 11 June 1944 at Le Château d'Audrieu near Mesnil-Patry and at Le Haut du Bosq. The monument was unveiled by a Canadian senator, Colonel the Honourable G. L. Molgat, on the 8 June 1989.

🔫 AUTHIE

Authie lies just to the north-west of Caen. To reach the village, leave the D22 at Buron and follow the D220 southwards for two kilometres.

The village marked the furthest point reached by the Canadians during the first six days after D-Day. It was in this area that on 7 June, units of the· Canadian 9th Infantry Brigade first came face-to-face with tanks of Colonel Kurt Meyer's 12th SS Panzers.

In the centre of the village directly opposite the Mairie is a monument which recalls that 'on June 7, 1944, in this town and in the surrounding fields, the North Nova Scotia Highlanders experienced their first baptism of fire. Eighty-four North Novas, and seven citizens of Authie, lost their lives this day'. It was later claimed that, although the Canadian 9th Infantry Brigade had fought its first battle 'with courage and spirit', it had nevertheless come off second best because its advanced guard 'had been caught off balance and defeated in detail'.

🔫 BANNEVILLE-LA-CAMPAGNE WAR CEMETERY

Banneville-la-Campagne is a village some ten kilometres east of Caen on the N175, the road which leads towards Troarn. The war cemetery lies about 450 metres west of the village on the south side of the road to Caen.

The cemetery contains 2,175 burials of which 2,150 are British and the remainder Canadian (11), Australian (5), New Zealand (2) and Polish (5). There are 147 graves of unidentified servicemen. The majority of the men were killed between the second week of July 1944 and the last week in August.

In the cemetery there are the graves of many men of the 5th Duke of Cornwall's Light Infantry who were killed on 11 July 1944 during the battle for Hill 112, later to be called 'Cornwall Hill'. Strategically important, the Germans were of the opinion that 'he who holds Hill 112 holds Normandy' and, on 11 July, launched no less than twelve counter-attacks against the positions held in an orchard by the DCLI. The 5th Battalion, threatened with annihilation, was forced to withdraw but not before they had suffered three hundred and twenty casualties of which only one was taken prisoner. There are also a large number of graves of men of the 4th Battalion Welsh Regiment killed on 23 July near Evrecy after the fall of Caen. Of the many decorated servicemen, two officers both awarded the Military Cross lie side by side – Captain Harold Woods of the Dorset and Hampshire Yeomanry (RA) and Major A. M. N. Rice of the Northamptonshire Regiment. Buried under adjacent headstones are the members of the crew of a Mitchell bomber that took off from RAF Dunsford on 23 July to attack German troop movements in the area of Coutances. The pilot, Flight Sergeant W.O. Worrall, and the three other members of his crew were killed when their aircraft was shot down.

BARFLEUR

The fishing port of Barfleur lies on the north-eastern corner of the Cotentin Peninsula. It can be approached directly from Cherbourg by driving twenty-seven kilometres east along the D901 or, if visiting Utah Beach, by travelling northward from Ravenoville along the D14 to Quettehou and then taking the D902 to the town.

The small port has a long and distinguished history. It was from here that, in 1066, William of Normandy set sail for England prior to his famous victory at Hastings. Henry I's only son, William, drowned here when his *White Ship* struck the treacherous rocks off Pointe de Barfleur in 1120. The naval battle of La Hogue between a combined Dutch and English fleet and a French fleet under Admiral de Tourville was fought off the same Pointe in 1692. Heavily fortified by the Germans, the port played no part in the events of D-Day, although its citizens must have enjoyed a grandstand view of what was happening to the south and east. Barfleur was finally liberated by the Americans on 21 June, nearly a week before the fall of Cherbourg.

Close to the port, though not easily accessible, there are the remains of several German bunkers. Inside the seventeenth-century church is a fine stained-glass window dedicated to the memory of the liberation of the port. While travelling along the Barfleur-Cherbourg coast road (D116), you may think it worthwhile visiting the remains of the impressive German battery and observation platform at Anse du Brick close to Mauperthuis. Although easily visible from the road, the climb is steep and the area around ruinous of one's clothes!

BASLY

Basly is a small village just to the south-west of Douvres-la-Délivrande and not far distant from the Canadian cemetery at Bény-sur-Mer. After leaving the cemetery turn right along the D404 for about five kilometres before turning to reach the village which again is on the right hand side. Alternatively take an earlier turning to Bény-sur-Mer and, after passing through the village, continue along the D79 to Basly.

The village was liberated by the Regiment de la Chaudière of the Canadian 3rd Infantry Division on 6 June 1944. On a roadside verge is an elegant maple-leaf shaped memorial which reads, 'Recollection and gratitude to the Canadian liberators. The 6th June 1944'.

In the village churchyard is the grave of one British soldier. Sergeant Alfred Barnes from Bamber Bridge in Lancashire served with The Black Watch and was killed on 17 June.

🪖 BAYEUX

The old and historical Norman town of Bayeux can be reached by following the N13 from Caen or by travelling south from Arromanches on the D516.

Long famous for its cathedral and tapestry, the capture of the town was the major objective of the British 50th Division on D-Day. Although the dash from the coast to the town went as planned and.the outskirts of the town were reached by the evening of D-Day, the advance British units hesitated to occupy the town in darkness and waited until the following morning. On 7 June 1944, Bayeux became the first sizeable town to be liberated after four years of German occupation. Fortunately the Germans had withdrawn and left the town undefended and this meant that, unlike most other towns in Calvados and Manche, Bayeux remained largely undamaged. On 14 June, General Charles de Gaulle entered the town in triumph. In the Place Charles de Gaulle, there is a monument which marks the place where the general made his first speech on liberated French soil. The town also has a museum dedicated to the leader of the Free French, the Institut Charles de Gaulle in Rue Bourbesneur.

The centre of the town, much of it now a pedestrian precinct, has changed little since the time of its liberation. In Rue Larcher, close to the post office, is a memorial to those who were deported and died in Nazi concentration camps. Follow the Rue Saint Malo and then the Rue Saint Patrice to reach the roundabout, the Rond Point de Vaucelles, on the exit to Cherbourg (N13). In the centre of the roundabout is the Monument de la Libération. It is said to be the only monument to portray General de Gaulle made during his lifetime. Along Boulevard Faben Ware, a section of the Bayeux ring-road, lie the 1944 Battle of Normandy Memorial Museum and the Bayeux British War Cemetery and Memorial. The Museum was specially designed to house this exhibition and it provides a detailed account of the events in Normandy from the landings in June to the closing of the Falaise gap in August. The Museum cinema shows archival films about the Battle of Normandy and, outside, there is a selection of Allied and German tanks and other armoured vehicles.

No tour of Bayeux would be complete without visiting the town's cathedral and the famous tapestry which both lie close to the centre of the town. The Cathedral of Notre Dame was completed in 1077 by Bishop Odo, William the Conqueror's half-brother. One of the most beautiful cathedrals in France, it is a superb monument to gothic architecture. In the cathedral there is a tablet to the memory of 'one million dead of the British Empire who fell in the Great War ... and of whom the greatest part rest in France'. Below is a memorial erected by the comrades of the 56th Infantry Brigade, British Liberation Army to those who 'died in the campaign for the liberation of North Western Europe – June 1944-May 1945'. There is also a stained-glass window dedicated to the men of the Allied sea, land and air forces who took part in the D-Day and Normandy operations. Outside, on a wall of the Ancien Hôtel du Doyen, is a memorial to all ranks of the 50th Northumbrian Division 'who laid down their lives for justice, freedom and the liberation of France in the assault on the beaches of La Rivière, Le Hamel and Arromanches on the 6th June 1944 and in the battles on the fields of Normandy'. It also records that 'the town of Bayeux was the first town in France to be liberated by the Allied armies and was entered and freed by troops of this Division on the morning of 7th June 1944'.

It was in Bayeux that Harold originally took an oath on saintly relics that on the death of Edward the Confessor he would support William of Normandy's claim to the throne of England. He went back on his word and this led to the Norman invasion in 1066. The whole story is told on the Bayeux Tapestry, which is now housed in the *Centre Guillaume le Conquérant* off the Rue de Nesmond. This masterpiece of embroidery tells the story of the Norman invasion of England in 1066 in fifty-eight episodes. Seventy metres long, it has been described as one of the oldest examples of a strip cartoon.

🐾 BAYEUX BRITISH WAR CEMETERY AND MEMORIAL

The British War Cemetery in Bayeux lies on the opposite side of the road to the museum, some two hundred metres further along the Bayeux ring road and just before you reach the junction with the D5, the road leading to Littry. It is the largest British and Commonwealth military cemetery of the Second World War to be found in France. After the war, burials were brought together from surrounding districts and hospitals and the cemetery now contains 4,648 graves including 3,935 British, 466 German, 25 Polish and 17 Australian as well as smaller numbers of Czech, French, Italian, Russian and South African servicemen. Among those buried there are Camberwell-born Corporal Sidney Bates of the Royal Norfolk Regiment who was awarded a VC for his bravery at Sourdeval on 8 August 1944; twenty-eight-year-old Lieutenant Colonel I. R. Woods, DSO, MC and Bar, commanding officer of the 9th Durham Light Infantry who fell in June 1944; and Major John Pooley MC, of No. 3 Commando, who was killed during the attack on the

Merville Battery just before dawn on 6 June. The cemetery also contains the grave of the sportsman, Major Maurice Turnbull of the Welsh Guards. Killed at Montchamp on 4 August 1944, Turnbull captained Cambridge University and Glamorgan in cricket and was the first Glamorgan player to win a Test Cap when he played against New Zealand in 1929. He was also a Welsh rugby international and represented his country in both hockey and squash.

Directly opposite, on the other side of the road, is the Bayeux Memorial. This was designed by Philip Hepworth and has engraved on it the names of the 1,808 men of Britain and the Commonwealth who fell in the Battle of Normandy and the following advance to the River Seine but who have no known grave. The Latin inscription on the frieze reads, *'NOS A GULIELMO VICTI VICTORIS PATRIAM LIBERAVIMUS'* ('We, once conquered by William, have now set free the Conqueror's native land'). Among those listed on the panel is Lieutenant Michael Dowling who lost his life during the assault on the Merville Battery on D-Day.

A small group of British soldiers are to be found in another cemetery in Bayeux. In the *Cimetière Saint Exupère*, next to the church St Exupère just off the Boulevard Montgomery, are the graves of a twenty-two-year-old officer of the Rifle Brigade, Major F. A. Dorrien Smith, two other officers and a rifleman of the same regiment and a REME corporal.

🐾 BAZENVILLE

About twelve kilometres to the north-east of Bayeux and close to Ryes War Cemetery lies the village of Bazenville. It can be reached by following the D12 from Bayeux to Sommervieu and from there taking the Dll2 to the point where it joins the D87. The village is on the right just beyond Ryes War Cemetery.

The village with its spired church receives little coverage in the annals of the D-Day landings but during the period 16 June to 15 August 1944 the fields around were the site of Bazenville aerodrome. This hastily built airfield was used by 403,416 and 421 Squadrons of the Royal Canadian Air Force. A plaque on the church wall close to the gate recalls this fact.

During the period immediately after D-Day numerous airfields had to be quickly constructed and made operational. The map showing the location and extent of the landing field, servicing and maintenance areas and other facilities required gives some idea of the upheaval it must have meant for the local farming community around Bazenville. Today there is little evidence that units of the Royal Canadian Air Force were ever based there.

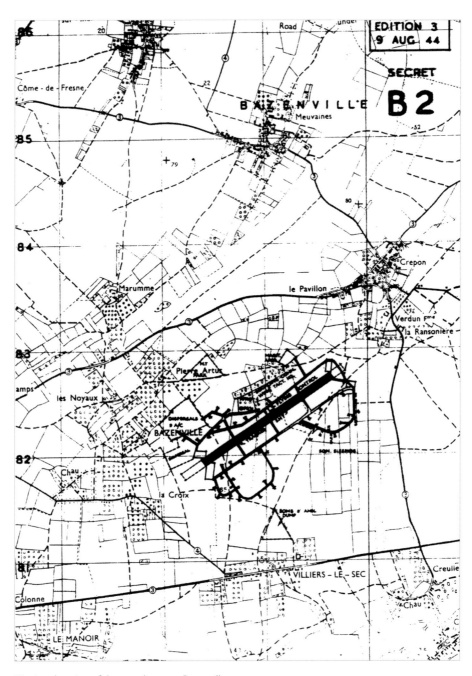

Wartime location of the aerodrome at Bazenville.

🐾 BÉNOUVILLE

Bénouville is on the west bank of the River Orne and lies just off the D514/D515, the dual carriageway linking the cross-Channel ferry port of Ouistreham and the city of Caen. Four kilometres outside Ouistreham, leave the dual carriageway and continue on the D514 towards the village and Pegasus Bridge.

Bénouville and its famous bridge over the River Orne are inextricably linked with the events of 5/6 June 1944. The first troops to land were those in the six gliders carrying the men of the 2nd Battalion the Oxfordshire and Buckinghamshire Light Infantry under Major John Howard. Shortly after midnight, they were followed by the paratroopers of the 7th Light Infantry Battalion, the Parachute Regiment. It was not until 3.00 a.m. that the 7th Parachute Battalion crossed the canal bridge and took up positions in Bénouville and Le Port. Then, wrote Sir Huw Wheldon (at that time a captain serving with the 6th Airborne Division and later to become Managing Director of BBC Television), they 'held these positions through a long and merciless day, under continuous shelling and in the teeth of a number of German attacks, until the arrival that evening of troops from the beaches who had landed that morning and fought their way inland:

At the crossroads in the village is the 'Mairie', with a plaque on the wall which claims that it was the first town hall to be liberated on D-Day when 'les parachutistes anglais' arrived at 11.45 p.m. on the evening of 5 June. Opposite is a memorial crucifix set against a stone wall which is inscribed '6th June, 1944' and below a memorial to the 7th Light Infantry Battalion of the Parachute Regiment, 'In memory of those who died holding this bridge-head, 6th June 1944'. The memorial is supported by a stone plinth marked 'Pax'. The road leading towards Pegasus Bridge is named 'Avenue du Commandant Kieffer' after the leader of the French Commandos.

In Bénouville there is also an eighteenth-century château. During the years of occupation, its owner, Madame Vion, had rigorously resisted German attempts to take over her home and, in June 1944, it was being run as a shelter for unmarried mothers. During the fighting on D-Day, Madame Vion provided British paratroopers with baths and drinking water.

Bénouville churchyard contains the graves of twenty-two British soldiers, the majority of whom belonged to the 6th Airborne Division. They include the Reverend George Parry from Leytonstone in Essex, an Army chaplain who was attached to the 7th Battalion of the Parachute Regiment. He was killed on D-Day.

🐾 BÉNY-SUR-MER

Bény-sur-Mer lies some four kilometres inland from Courseulles-sur-Mer on the D79. Alternatively follow the D79 from Caen and the village is three kilometres beyond Basly.

Above: The remains of one of the Merville Battery casemates today.

Right: British troops landing from LCMs at Asnelles.

British troops and a Bren-gun carrier in the streets of Hermanville.

Allied tanks rumble through the streets of La Délivrande on 8 June.

General Montgomery in Port-en-Bessin on 10 June.

Left: Company Sergeant Major Stanley Hollis VC.
Right: Corporal Sidney Bates VC.

Above left: Captain David Jamieson VC.
Above right: Lieutenant Tasker Watkins VC.
Left: Major David Currie VC.

The stone of remembrance at Bény-sur-Mer (Reviers) Canadian War Cemetery.

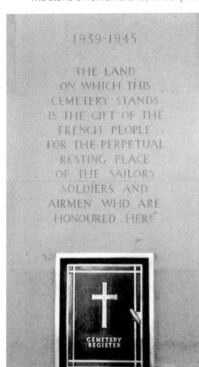

1939-1945

THE LAND
ON WHICH THIS
CEMETERY STANDS
IS THE GIFT OF THE
FRENCH PEOPLE
FOR THE PERPETUAL
RESTING PLACE
OF THE SAILORS
SOLDIERS AND
AIRMEN WHO ARE
HONOURED HERE

CEMETERY
REGISTER

JEFFERSON, Cpl. NORMAN, 7013019. 1st (Airborne) Bn. The Royal Ulster Rifles. 7th June, 1944. Age 26. Son of Thomas and Sarah Jefferson, of Lisburn, Co. Down, Northern Ireland. IIA. C. 5.

JEFFERY, L. Bdr. ALFRED WALTER, 816998. 107 H.A.A. Regt., Royal Artillery. 28th July, 1944. Age 30. Son of Arthur and Alice Jeffery; husband of Edna I. Jeffery, of Eastry, Kent. III. A. 26.

JEFFERY, Pte. THOMAS, 6211305. 2nd Bn. The Middlesex Regt. 6th June, 1944. Age 24. Son of Thomas Edward and Thurzza Jeffery, of Shildon, Co. Durham. III. A. 9.

JENKINS, Sjt. WILLIE, 2649323. 12 Ordnance Base Depot, R.A.O.C. 7th June, 1944. Age 31. Son of Tom and Louisa Jenkins, of Wyke, Bradford, Yorkshire; husband of Nellie Jenkins, of Wyke. II. D. 5.

JENKINSON, Pte. THOMAS, 14429835. 5th Bn. The Black Watch (Royal Highland Regt.). 11th June, 1944. Age 19. Son of John and Annie Jenkinson, of Halsell, Lancashire. VA. M. 4.

JEPP, Pte. RONALD SYDNEY, 5511515. 9th Bn. The Parachute Regt., A.A.C. 12th June, 1944. Age 20. Son of Edward Walter and Doris Vera Jepp, of Southsea, Hampshire. IA. G. 15.

JESTICO, Sjt. STANLEY WILLIAM, T/113247. R.A.S.C., attd. 507th Inf. Bde. 25th July, 1944. Age 25. Son of Harry and Clara Alice Jestico, of Hunston, Sussex. IVA. D. 1.

JEVONS, L. Cpl. JOHN STANLEY, 7348925. 33 Field Dressing Station, R.A.M.C. 3rd August, 1944. Age 23. Son of George and Mary E. Jevons, of Liverpool. IV. C. 19.

JOHANNESSEN, Tpr. NORMAN ERNEST, 3862633. 148th (9th Bn. The Loyal Regt. [North Lancashire]) Regt., R.A.C. 11th July, 1944. Age 24. Son of George and Maud Johannessen, of Grassendale, Lancashire. VIII. B. 4.

JOHNS, Pte. ROBERT EDWARD, 14434704. 13th (2/4th Bn. The South Lancashire Regt.) Bn. The Parachute Regt., A.A.C. 23rd July, 1944. Age 16. Son of William Henry and Daisy Nellie Johns, of Stamshaw, Portsmouth. IVA. E. 1.

JOHNS, Rfn. WILLIAM HENRY, 7022700. 1st (Airborne) Bn. The Royal Ulster Rifles. 7th June, 1944. Age 23. Son of Henry H. J. and Elizabeth M. Johns, of Waddon, Croydon, Surrey. IA. L. 17.

JOHNSON, Pte. ALBERT EDWARD, 4860768. 1st Bn. The Leicestershire Regt. 8th August, 1944. Age 26. Son of George Herbert Johnson, and of Miriam Jane Johnson, of Leicester. I. D. 34.

JOHNSON, Lt.-Col. ALEXANDER PERCIVAL, 52653, D.S.O. The Suffolk Regt. Cdg. 12th (10th Bn. The Green Howards [Yorkshire Regt.]) Bn. The Parachute Regt., A.A.C. 12th June, 1944. Age 32. Son of Colonel Henry Alexander Johnson and Constance Bertha Johnson; husband of Jeanne Heléne Johnson, of Camberley, Surrey. IVA. C. 10.

JOHNSON, Sjt. ANDREW WILLIAM TEASDALE, 1423440. 143 (The Kent Yeomanry) Field Regt., Royal Artillery. 30th July, 1944. Age 40. Son of Andrew Neil and Harriet Johnson; husband of Agnes Medice Johnson, of Earlsfield, London. III. C. 10.

JOHNSON, L. Cpl. BERNARD GEORGE, 7905991. 1st The Northamptonshire Yeomanry, R.A.C. 15th August, 1944. Age 25. Son of Thomas and Minnie Florence Johnson, of Northampton; husband of Edna Lilian Johnson. IX. F. 28.

JOHNSON, Pte. CHARLES ALFRED, B/47149. 1st Canadian Parachute Bn., R.C.I.C. 19th June, 1944. Age 20. Son of Charles F. and Anna May Johnson, of Toronto, Ontario, Canada. IA. C. 9.

JOHNSON, Pte. DENNIS, 14405715. 8th Bn. The Parachute Regt., A.A.C. 6th June, 1944. Son of Charles Edward and Daisy Elizabeth Johnson, of Welford-on-Avon, Warwickshire. Coll. grave V. B. 1-22.

JOHNSON, L. Cpl. JOHN THOMAS CARR, 4341055. 2nd Bn. The East Yorkshire Regt. 6th June, 1944. Age 33. Son of John and Jane Ann Johnson, of Newcastle-on-Tyne; husband of Agnes Good Martin Johnson, of Heaton, Newcastle-on-Tyne. III. D. 5.

JOHNSON, Cpl. KENNETH FRANK, 5392120. 2nd (Airborne) Bn. The Oxfordshire and Buckinghamshire Light Infantry. 15th June, 1944. Age 20. Son of Frank William and Gladys Johnson, of Hall Green, Birmingham. IA. H. 22.

JOHNSON, L. Sjt. RICHARD HENRY, 1875657. 17 Field Coy., Royal Engineers. 8th June, 1944. Age 24. Son of William and Elizabeth Johnson, of Birr, Co. Offaly, Irish Republic. II. C. 14.

JOHNSON, Pte. THOMAS HARRY, 4696371. 13th (2/4th The South Lancashire Regt.) Bn. The Parachute Regt., A.A.C. 6th June, 1944. Age 29. Son of Henry and Edith Johnson; husband of Gladys May Johnson, of Driffield, Yorkshire. IIA. L. 10.

RANVILLE WAR CEMETERY PR. 1071

47

Left: A war cemetery register.

Right: A page from a war cemetery register.

Examples of Service and Regimental insignia and badges on headstones of the Commonwealth War Graves Commission:

Top left: Royal Navy.

Above: Royal Air Force.

Left: Welsh Guards.

Below left: Parachute Regiment.

General de Gaulle making his famous speech on his arrival in Bayeux.

The tablet in the centre of the Monument de la Libération in Bayeux, showing General de Gaulle being welcomed in the town.

Above: The Bayeux Memorial to the 1,808 British and Commonwealth servicemen who have no known graves.

Left: Major Maurice Turnbull. the England cricketer and Welsh rugby international, who lies in the Bayeux cemetery.

Below left: Lieutenant Michael Dowling, who lost his life during the assault on the Merville Battery. His name is listed on the Bayeux Memorial.

The village was liberated by the Canadian 3rd Infantry Division's Regiment de la Chaudière during the afternoon of D-Day and, in the centre of the village, immediately in front of the church, there is a memorial tablet which reads, '*Reconnaissance aux soldats Canadiens du Régiment de la Chaudière qui libérerent ce village 6 Juin 1944*'. Close to the village at the D79/D404 crossroads is a memorial which records the fact that the area thereabout was the site of an aerodrome used by 301, 311 and 412 Squadrons of the Royal Canadian Air Force during the period 18 June to 7 August 1944.

BÉNY-SUR-MER CANADIAN WAR CEMETERY

To visit the Canadian War Cemetery, leave the village on the D79 and then turn on to the D35 towards Reviers. The Cemetery, which is actually closer to Reviers than Bény-sur-Mer, is to be found one kilometre away on the right-hand side of the road at the highest and probably most windswept point around.

This impressive War Cemetery contains the graves of 2,048 servicemen of whom all but about five are Canadians. They were killed during the period of the Normandy landings and the early stages of the fighting for Caen. Each side of the approach to the graves is a watch-tower. In the one on the left-hand side is a memorial plaque to the Cameron Highlanders of Ottawa.

🐾 BERNIÈRES-SUR-MER

Bernières-sur-Mer lies on the coastal road, the D514, midway between Courseulles-sur-Mer and St Aubin-sur-Mer.

On 6 June this coastal resort marked the centre of the Nan sector of Juno Beach, the area of assault allocated to the Canadian 8th Infantry Brigade which was part of the Canadian 3rd Infantry Division. At 8.15 a.m., the first unit to land was the Queen's Own Rifles of Canada. The sea was too rough for amphibious tanks to land and the Regiment found itself struggling through German beach obstacles which were virtually intact and subjected to the most murderous small-arms fire from machine-gun nests. It lost half its number covering the 100 metres from the landing craft to the relative safety of the sea wall. The situation was in part saved through the courage of a ship's officer who brought his craft close inshore and riddled the German strong-point with anti-aircraft shells. During the course of the day, the casualties of the Queen's Own Rifles exceeded that of any other Canadian unit. They were followed ashore by the French-Canadian Régiment de la Chaudière and together they fought their way inland towards Bény-sur-Mer until the intensity of the German resistance was such that the advance ground to a halt. As a result there was a pile-up on the beaches as men and equipment continued to pour ashore.

Along the seafront and raised on a triangular base there is a *Comité du Débarquement* memorial which records that 'Here on the 6th June 1944 Europe was liberated by the heroism of the Allied forces'. Two hundred metres further along in the Place du Canada is the former German bunker bearing a memorial to the Queen's Own Rifles of Canada and just beyond that an impressive stone memorial to the Regiment de la Chaudière du Canada and its commander, Lieutenant Colonel Paul Mathieu. In the town, the Hôtel de Grave in the Rue du Régiment de la Chaudière has a plaque which commemorates the fact that after D-Day the hotel was the first head-quarters of war correspondents and film crews and it was from here that the first on-the-spot reports of the D-Day landings were dictated.

🐾 BRETTEVILLE L'ORGUELLLEUSE

Bretteville-l'Orgueilleuse lies just off the N13 on the D83. The straggling village is eleven kilometres to the west of Caen and sixteen kilometres to the east of Bayeux.

By the evening of D-Day, the leading units of the Canadian 3rd Infantry Division had reached the village as they edged their way towards Caen.

In the village square and opposite the post office is an elegant memorial to The Regina Rifle Regiment which is inscribed *'N'oublie pas Juin 1944'*. Close by is the local war memorial dedicated *'Aux enfants de Bretteville morts pour la France'*. On the reverse side it lists those from the village who lost their lives during the Second World War. The memorial indicates the extent of the contribution made by the Lecanu family in both wars. In addition to the parts played by Raymond Lecanu and his brothers in the Second World War (see Brouay and Brouay War Cemetery) two other members of the family fell during the 1914–18 war.

🐾 BRÉVILLE-LES-MONTS

Bréville lies to the east of the estuary of the River Orne twelve kilometres north-east of Caen and five kilometres south of Merville-Franceville Plage. After crossing Pegasus Bridge follow the D514 for some four kilometres before turning to the right to reach the village of Amfreville. Bréville is only a short drive ahead along the D236.

Because the village was on high ground with the outskirts of Caen clearly visible in the distance, it was of considerable strategic importance and was heavily defended. It was to be the scene of some of the most ferocious fighting during the post-D-Day period. The capture of the town was first allocated to the 3rd Parachute Brigade of the 6th Airborne Division who landed near the village on the night of 5/6 June. Unfortunately their assault got bogged down and by 10 June the village was still held by the Germans. As the days passed, enemy pressure threatened to create a dangerous gap in the perimeter and endanger the whole left flank and it became increasingly urgent that the high ground be taken. On 11 June, the paratroopers, reinforced by the 5th Black Watch, carried out a further assault but again it failed. The Black Watch, in experiencing their first taste of battle, suffered two hundred casualties but 'Every man of the leading platoon died with his face to the foe.' The following day it was the turn of the 12th Parachute Regiment, the 12th Devons and the tanks of the 13th/18th Hussars. Unfortunately the supporting artillery barrage fell short and this caused casualties and created some confusion among the advancing troops. It is possible that Lord Lovat, who was wounded at this time, fell victim to what we today call 'friendly fire'. The battle, 'more a matter of necessity than of policy', proved expensive to both sides. A total of 141 of the 160 paratroopers who took part in the assault became casualties, while the price of defending the village cost the Germans 418 out of their 564 men, but at the end of the day the village was in British hands. Afterwards, the 12th Devons took over positions in the grounds of the Château St Côme which lies some 400 metres to the south-east of the village. This fine example of a small château had once been a famous racing stud where some of the finest French racing stock was bred. Now, after the area had been bitterly contested, the stables were reduced to rubble and many of the horses killed. Jeremy Taylor, historian of the Devonshire Regiment, described the situation: '... a sweet stench of the decaying bodies set the atmosphere of the place. Yellowing corpses of German soldiers lay where they had fallen in hand-to-hand combat, amid charred carriers and already rusting weapons.'

The war chronicle of the Oxfordshire and Buckinghamshire Light Infantry records, 'It was pathetic to see wounded mares and fouls struggling in the fields, and somewhat precarious, in the early stages, to go to help them owing to the presence of enemy snipers. The value of the horses destroyed must have been very great.'

Today Bréville remains a fairly typical Norman village centred on its church and common. Opposite the church is a memorial to the 12th Battalions of both the Parachute and Devonshire Regiments who 'on the evening of 12th June 1944 assaulted through the 1st Commando Brigade positions from the direction of Amfreville and drove out the German force.'

In the church cemetery and hidden away among the civilian graves are the headstones of two British soldiers – Private Charles Masters of the 12th Battalion, The Parachute Regiment, who came from Ilchester in Somerset, and thirty-four-year-old Captain H. W. Ward of the 53rd (Worcestershire Yeomanry) Airlanding Light Regiment R.A. Both men were killed on 12 June.

To reach the Château St Côme, follow the D375 south for some four hundred metres. Outside the perimeter fence is a monument to the 9th Parachute Battalion which provides details of the Battle of Les Bois des Monts and the Château St Côme during the period 7-13 June 1944.

🐾 BROUAY

The village of Brouay lies just off the N13, midway between Caen and Bayeux. Leave the dual carriageway after about ten kilometres and follow the D94 through Putot-en-Bessin and then on to Brouay. To reach the war cemetery, at the village centre turn right and follow the road under the railway arch until you see the church straight ahead.

BROUAY WAR CEMETERY

This lies on raised ground at the rear of the church and you have to pass through the churchyard to reach it. The cemetery contains the graves of 377 men who, apart from two Canadians, are all British. The men were involved in the heavy fighting during June and July 1944 when the British forces attempted to swing to the south of Caen from the west. There are a number of troopers of the 1st East Riding Yeomanry (Royal Armoured Corps) who were all killed on 7 June. The headstone of Troop Sergeant Thomas Duke of Hull carries the touching epitaph, 'Deep in our hearts a memory is kept, of one we loved dearly and will never forget.' There are also many graves of men of the Oxfordshire and Buckinghamshire Light Infantry who fell on 16 July and, unusually, seven lance-corporals of the 53rd Division Provost Company, Corps of Military Police, who were killed on 21 July. High on the bank, one section of the cemetery might be referred to as 'Welsh Corner' since the graves there are mainly of men who served in the Royal Welch Fusiliers, the South Wales Borderers, the Welch Regiment and the Monmouthshire Regiment.

Alongside the path in the churchyard and part of a cluster of family graves is a memorial to a nineteen-year-old Frenchman, Raymond Lecanu. He was one of the three sons of a baker from Bretteville-l'Orgueilleuse who all played an active part in the war. The eldest brother, Roger, a minesweeper and took part in the D-Day operations. Like many Frenchmen, a second brother, Louis, left the region when called up for 'le service du travail obligatoire' – deportation for forced labour – and joined the Maquis. Ten days afterwards, the third brother, Raymond, was arrested by the Gestapo together with other members of the local Resistance. Held in turn in Caen, Paris and Compiègne, the men were tortured before being sent to Stutthof concentration camp. Raymond Lecanu was later transferred to Dachau where he died on 9 September 1944. As his brother, Louis, says, he was 'parmi celle des autres camarades morts pour la liberté' (among those other comrades who died for freedom).

🐾 BURON

Buron lies just to the north-west of Caen. The village is easily reached by driving some nine kilometres north-westwards out of the city along the D22.

After fierce house-to-house fighting involving the North Nova Scotia Highlanders and the 27th Armoured Regiment (Sherbrooke Fusiliers), Buron was first liberated on 7 June by the Canadians advancing inland from Juno Beach. On the afternoon of the same day, the Germans counter-attacked and managed to retake the village. Canadian losses were heavy and aggravated by rumours that prisoners-of-war had been shot by fanatical teenage members of the 12th SS (Hitler Youth) Panzer Division. It was not until the morning of the 8 July that the British and Canadians combined to move towards Buron as part of a more general advance on Carpiquet. Again the fighting was ferocious, with the Highland Light Infantry suffering heavy casualties, but, during the morning of the following day, German resistance finally came to an end.

After the war, Colonel Kurt Meyer, who commanded the 12th SS (Hitler Youth) Panzer Division, was found guilty by a Canadian Military Court of charges relating to the murder of twenty-three Canadians at Buron on 7 June and sentenced to be shot. Described as 'tall and stiffly handsome, he was the archetype of the Nazi lunatic.' His sentence was commuted to life imprisonment but he was released after nine years.

Today the events of June/July 1944 are recalled by two memorials. In the main square, the Place des Canadiens, there is a memorial to the Highland Infantry of Canada who were 'among the first Allied troops to enter Caen' and another to the Sherbrooke Fusiliers. To find 'Hell's Corner' memorial to the Canadian 9th Infantry Brigade, leave the village, cross the D22 and then proceed along the D75 for a short distance. The men of that Brigade fought in the area during the month following the 7 June.

🐾 CAEN

Caen, a large and rapidly growing industrial city and port, is the capital of lower Normandy. It can be reached directly by driving fourteen kilometres along the D514 and DS15 from the ferry port of Ouistreham. It is 119 kilometres from Cherbourg and 107 from Le Havre.

The capture of Caen had been one of the intended major objectives on D-Day but such an advance proved over-ambitious. Even with the Normandy beaches cleared, German counter-attacks beaten off and the Allied armies moving inland, it was going to take a further two months of bitter fighting before the city finally fell. Caen was to become a fiercely contested battleground where the British and Canadians would struggle to contain concentrations of German Panzers grouped around the city and so create an opportunity for the American 1st Army to swing southwards and break out towards St Lô and then into the interior of France. On 26 June, British troops launched Operation *Epsom*, a drive against Caen from the west. The very nature of the wooded and hedged *bocage* countryside made the going difficult and gradually the offensive ground to a halt. In places, the situation reached stalemate and the ensuing war of attrition proved costly to both sides. Heavy Allied bombing reached a new ferocity on the night of 7 July when, as a prelude to Operation *Charnwood*, the final assault on the city, more than a thousand Lancasters and Halifaxes of RAF Bomber Command dropped 2,200 tonnes of bombs on its northern outskirts. Even though three-quarters of Caen was razed to the ground, much of the bombing was off target and inflicted only negligible damage on the German defences.

On 8 July the British began to fight their way into the city and faced fanatical opposition from the *'Hitler Jugend'* members of the 12th SS Panzer Division. The Canadians, who had succeeded in liberating Carpiquet on the 9 July, now moved into the city from the west. Two days of savage house-to-house fighting followed before the parts of the city on the west bank of the River Orne were in Allied hands. It took ten more days before Vaucelles, a suburb on the east bank, finally fell. The city was not completely liberated until the 20 July and, even then, it remained within the range of German guns for another month. During the period of the battle, the people of Caen found refuge wherever they could. Some 1,500 sheltered in the *Abbay aux Hommes (Église Saint-Étienne)*, another four thousand in the hospice of *Bon Sauveur* and some in the quarries at Fleury where whole families lived together like troglodytes. Even so, there were some three thousand civilian victims of the battle. The Malberbe school was turned into a hospital where the refectory served as an operating theatre and the dead were buried in the courtyards.

In spite of extensive war damage which included the destruction of the city's centre and the total or partial demolition of fourteen thousand houses. Caen emerged from its ruins to become once again an important and historical city with a great deal to interest visitors. In the centre of the city stands the remains of the château built by William of Normany and his son Henry. Within its impressive ramparts are to be found the *Esplanade de la Paix* and two museums, the *Musée des Beaux-Arts* and the *Musée de Normandie*. In St George's Chapel there is a memorial to the civilians who died in the Battle for Caen. Off the *Rue Guillaume-le-Conquérant* lies the ancient *Abbaye aux Hommes* which includes the *Église St Étienne*. Here, where so many found shelter in July 1944, is the tomb of its founder, William the Conqueror. Some distance away on the eastern side of the château and at the end of the *Rue des Chanoines* is the *Abbaye aux Dames* with the *Église de la Trinité*. The abbey was founded by Queen Matilda, the Conequeror's wife, and her mausoleum is in the centre of the choir. The *Église St Pierre*, a church strikingly rich in its adornment, was badly damaged on 13 July when a shell from HMS *Rodney* sent its spire crashing to the floor.

The city contains a great many memorials and monumnets. On the wall of the *Préfecture* in the *Boulevard Bertrand* is a memorial to the first Canadian soldier to fall during the liberation of Caen; within the château, there are plaques in honour of the men and women of the Province of Ontario who served in the Canadian armed forces and to General Charles de Gaulle, *'Libérateur de la France'*. At the foot of the

CAPTURE OF CAEN

———◆———

CITY TAKEN BY BRITISH AND CANADIANS

————

MASSIVE ASSAULT FROM AIR, SEA, AND LAND

————

LA HAYE DU PUITS FALLS TO AMERICANS

British and Canadian forces of the Second Army have captured Caen after a massive assault from air, sea, and land. The Germans fought bitterly before the city was entered, and many pockets of resistance remain to be cleared, but last night's official report states that these are being systematically dealt with.

At the other end of the front the important communications centre of La Haye du Puits has fallen to the Americans.

A THREE-PRONGED ATTACK

———◆———

SECOND ARMY'S ACHIEVEMENT

————

CAEN HEAVILY MINED

From Our Special Correspondent
CAEN FRONT, July 9

What may turn out to be one of the most decisive battles in the liberation of France, the battle for Caen, is ebbing to its remorseless close—a remorselessness of power and finality that have marked each of General Montgomery's thrusts into the fair land of Normandy.

The battle was virtually won yesterday by British and Canadian formations who struck in three prongs from the north-west astride the roads that flow into the town like rivulets into a lake. It was indeed a day of achievement for the Second Army, and for the covering wings that dominated the sky. This was not a rout of half-hearted mercenaries. This time the Germans themselves were challenged and fought back into the streets of Caen over open ridges and cornfields, through the woods and valleys, in which defensive works of every contrivance formed a ring of steel round the place. By nightfall an S.S. Panzer division and a field division committed to coastal defence were broken.

Fall of Caen reported in *The Times* on 10 July.

steps leading to the battlement there is an unusual memorial to the *'soldats de la 3ème division d'infanterie Britannique. L'une des divisions d'assaut qui débarquèrent le 6 juin 1944 et libèrèrent Caen le 9 juillet 1944.'*

Just off the ring-road, the N13, in the *Esplanade Dwight Eisenhower* is the *Memorial – Un Musée Pour la Paix*. This museum, opened on 6 June 198 by President Mitterrand, is without doubt among the most impressive of those dedicated to the Second World War to be found anywhere in the world. The museum covers not just the events of the war and D-Day but, in addition, considers in the inter-war years and the events which led to the rise of the European dictators. Around the reception area there is a well stocked souvenir sand book shop, rest area and cloakrooms while upstairs there is a library and research room as well as a caféteria and bar. The museum itself is spread over three floors and there is a cinema/audio-visual room. Outside there is a *Vallée du Memorial* and, below the car park, a memorial to Frenchmen shot by the Germans while held in Cae prison. In order to do the museum justice, a minimum of two hours should be set aside for a visit.

CAMBES-EN-PLAINE

To reach Cambes-en-Plaine, leave Courseulles-sur-Mer on the D79 and travel towards Caen for some twelve kilometres. The village lies off that road between Villons-les-Buissons and Maton.

By 5 July, Cambes-en-Plaine was in the front line as the British 3rd Infantry Division hammered away at the Germans as they fought tenaciously to hold the hinge of their line, the city of Caen. In order to put an end to this resistance and make possible an Allied break-out to the south, Montgomery planned an all-out attack to the north and west of the city – Operation *Charnwood*. After a series of heavy air attacks and an initial artillery bombardment, the assault was to be carried out by men of the British 59th Infantry Division with the Canadian 3rd Infantry Division to the west and, to the east, the British 3rd Infantry Division. 'H' hour was set for 4.20 a.m. on the morning of 8 July. As the 6th North Staffords moved against La Bijude, so the 2/6th South Staffords attacked Galmanche, a village which was defended by units of the 12th SS Panzer Division. Throughout the day, the fighting was ferocious as advances made had to be held against a series of determined enemy counter attacks. Casualties were extremely heavy. As the British 59th Division made slow progress in the centre, so the Canadian 3rd and British 3rd Divisions on the flanks took advantage of the situation to advance into the outskirts of Caen.

Fighting continued into the next morning, the 9 July, as the 6th North Staffords cleared the area to the west of La Bijude and then occupied Malon. By this time, with British and Canadians fighting to clear the city, the Battle of Caen was drawing to its close. By 10 July, the greater part of the city was in Allied hands.

CAMBES-EN-PLAINE WAR CEMETERY

To find the British War Cemetery at Cambes-en-Plaine, leave the D79 and join the D79B which brings you to the village centre, opposite the church. Turn left and then, after five hundred metres, turn right. The Cemetery is 350 metres along on the right-hand side.

With some justification, the Cemetery might be called the 'Staffordshire Cemetery', since more than half the 224 burials here are of men of the South and North Staffordshire Regiments who fell during the bitter fighting for Caen on the 8 and 9 July 1944. On the grave of nineteen-year-old Private Reginald Parker, a South Stafford from Kendal in Westmorland, his parents poignantly comment, 'Goodnight, Reggie, some day maybe we'll understand'.

Raymond Lecanu, the young Resistance hero who was arrested and tortured by the Germans and who later died in Dachau concentration camp. His memorial is in the cemetery in Brouay.

The Fort du Roule situated above Cherbourg's inner harbour. It is easy to appreciate the strategic importance of the German strongpoint.

German soldiers relax in front of the Basilique Ste-Trinité in Cherbourg.

Looking eastward across Gold beach from a hilltop near St Côme de Fresné.

Juno beach, looking from Courseulles-sur-Mer towards Bernières-sur-Mer.

Looking across towards Sword, with Ouistreham in the distance.

Stone memorials of the Comité du Débarquement. set up in 1945 to preserve and dedicate the sites of the D-Day landings. in *above* Carentan and *below* Vierville-sur-Mer.

The Crisbeq Battery overlooked the American landing areas along Utah beach. The battery was finally overrun on 12 June.

The Longues Battery was sitated at the western end of Gold beach. It fell to the British troops advancing from Arromanches on 7 June.

The Merville Battery lay to the east of the Orne estuary and its guns were thought to be ranged on Sword beach. After fierce fighting, it was finally captured by British commandos on 7 June. The casemate has now been converted to a museum.

Left: A memorial to Commandant Kieffer on the sea-front at Ouistreham.

Above: Commandant Philippe Kieffer, the daring leader of French No. 7 and No. 8 troops which served with No. 4 Commando.

Today the dunes at Omaha beach are tranquil and deserted.

The National Guard Monument at Plage de Vierville-sur-Mer.

Ranville War Cemetery contains 2,563 burials, a great many of which are of men of the British 6th Airborne Division.

Above: Lieutenant Den Brotheridge, the first British soldier to be killed on D-Day.

Left: His grave lies in the churchyard adjoining Ranville War Cemetery.

🐾 CARENTAN

The town of Carentan lies on the N13 between Isigny-sur-Mer and St Côme-du-Mont and is some thirteen kilometres south of Ste Mère-Église. The town is at the base of the Cotentin Peninsula close to the point where the River Douve forms an estuary across low marshlands before it reaches the sea.

At the neck of the Cotentin Peninsula, the capture of Carentan was of particular importance since the town was situated astride the main road north to Cherbourg and at a point where the Peninsula was only fifty kilometres wide. Here it was intended that the US 101st Airborne Division advancing south from its landing area close to Ste Mère-Église would link up with the US 29th Division moving west from Omaha Beach. Once the town was secure and the divisions strengthened by follow-up units, the American forces would press forward and cut off the Peninsula. The capture of Carentan proved difficult for 101st Airborne Division. The approach to the town passed through the flat, waterlogged fields close to the Rivers Douve and Merderet and the enemy had blocked the main road across. Major von der Heydte and his 6th German Parachute Regiment fought doggedly and it took the Americans five days to clear the town. This done, they immediately faced a series of ferocious counter-attacks by the 17th SS Panzer Grenadier Division. The German onslaught very nearly succeeded and it was. the timely arrival of the tanks of the US 2nd Armoured Division from Isigny that saved the day. While the town was first liberated on 12 June, Carentan was not firmly in American hands until there had been a further two days of bitter fighting.

The poem 'Carentan O Carentan' by the American, Louis Simpson, gives some impression of the struggle for the town:

Carentan

There is a whistling in the leaves
And it is not the wind
The twigs are falling from the knives
That cut men to the ground.

Tell me, Master-Sergeant,
The way to turn an' shoot,
But the Sergeant's silent
That taught me how to do it.

Lieutenant, what's my duty,
My place in my platoon?

MR. CHURCHILL AT THE BEACH-HEAD

◆

VISIT WITH GENERAL SMUTS

FOREST OF CÉRISY IN AMERICAN HANDS

CAPTURE OF CARENTAN

Mr. Churchill, accompanied by General Smuts and General Sir Alan Brooke, Chief of the Imperial General Staff, visited the beach-head in Normandy yesterday. General Eisenhower, General Marshall, Admiral King, and General Arnold during the day toured the American sector of the beach-head.

Headlines in *The Times* on 13 June 1944

He too's a sleeping beauty,
Charmed by that strange tune.

Carentan O Carentan
Before we met with you
We never yet had lost a man
Or known what death could do

Captain, show us quickly
Our place upon the map
But the Captain's sickly
And taking a long nap

Although the town was severely damaged in June 1944, there remains little evidence today of those events. Several of the older buildings, such as the impressive church of *Notre Dame,* show evidence of shell damage and the town's memorial to the fallen of 1914-18 includes a panel dedicated *'aux victimes de la guerre 1939-1945'* and below are listed the names of the civilian victims of the struggle for the town. Outside the town hall there is a Comité du Débarquement monument commemorating the town's liberation and, at its base, a plaque presented by the 101st Airborne Division Association in honour 'of those "Screaming Eagles" who gave their lives in this campaign'.

CARPIQUET

Carpiquet lies just off the N13, immediately to the west of Caen, and includes the airport to the city.

Although advanced units of the North Nova Scotia Highlanders and the Sherbrook Fusiliers reached the outskirts of Carpiquet on the evening of D-Day, the snarl-up on the beaches at Bernières made it impractical for the Canadians to advance further. Had this been possible, the whole story of the desperate battle to take Caen might have been very different. As it was, the 12th SS Panzer Division was allocated to defend the small town and its airport and these diehard German troops resisted any advance for a further month. Early on the morning of 8 July a combined British and Canadian assault was launched towards Caen and Carpiquet fell to the Canadians on the following day.

There are two memorials at the roadside (D9). One placed on a ruined porchway in June 1982 is inscribed *'En souvenir du 4 Juillet 1944. Hommage de la commune de Carpiqet à ses Libérateurs Canadiens'.* The other is dedicated to the memory of the 'officers and men of the North Shore New Brunswick Regiment, 3rd Canadian Division, and the people of Normandy, who gave their lives during World War II'.

CHEF-DU-PONT

Chef-du-Pont is a hamlet just to the south-west of Ste Mère-Église. Leave the centre of Ste Mère-Église on the D67 and pass under the bridge beneath the N13 and proceed for just three kilometres.

Chef-du-Pont was in the centre of Zone 'N', the dropping zone allocated to the 508th Parachute Regiment of the US 82nd Airborne Division on the morning of D-Day. They had the misfortune to land in an area defended by the German 91st Division and, even worse, many men landed in the flooded fields close to the River Merderet and, weighed down by their heavy equipment, drowned. It was during this time that Maurice Duboscq, a French railwayman who managed Level Crossing 104, used his boat to rescue American paratroopers from the waters. On the D70, another road leading to the village from Les Forges, is a marker of former US Cemetery Number 2 which once contained the graves of six thousand American soldiers. Today, the fields close to the River Merderet are still often flooded. The river itself attracts not only fishermen but also groups of sub-aqua divers who are still able to find the debris of war on the river bed. By the bridge over the river is a monument to the 508th American Parachute Regiment.

The signal-box home of 'Papa Maurice' has now been demolished. You may think it worthwhile retracing your steps to Ste Mère-Église and then driving three kilometres along the DI5 to the bridge over the River Merderet at La Fière. Here at the roadside is the fox-hole of General James Gavin – still remarkably well preserved after fifty years! Out of the way but still quite easily reached from Chef-du-Pont is the memorial to the first American general to be killed during the Normandy campaign. Leave the village on the D70 and travel for nine kilometres until you reach a crossroads. Turn right along the D129 and continue until you come to a road junction and the turning to Hiesville. Here, set back from the road, is the memorial to Brigadier General Don F. Pratt. The assistant divisional commander of 101st US Airborne Division was killed before dawn on D-Day when his glider crashed a short distance away.

In his book *Airborne Warfare*, General Gavin recalls his experiences in the area:

> As darkness descended, I moved up to see what the situation looked like. The 1st Battalion of the 505th had taken heavy casualties. It was well organized and had the situation in hand, but the German defenses on the causeway seemed quite strong and there was no way to force a crossing of the causeway that night. From the causeway a road went directly back to the east, to our rear, to the town of Ste Mère-Église, about five miles away. I went back to where the road crossed the railroad and decided that I would establish my Command Post there. In that way I could control the situation at the causeway and stay in touch with the 507th at Chef-du-Pont. I established contact with division headquarters.

🐾 CHERBOURG

Cherbourg, a port with both trans-Atlantic and cross-Channel ferry inks, lies at the head of the Cotentin Peninsula. It can be approached rom several directions – from the south on the N13 from Valognes, along the D901 from Cap de la Hague in the west and from east on the D901 from Barfleur.

It is a little-known fact that there as the BEF was being evacuated from the beaches at Dunkirk during early June 1940, the vanguard of a Second BEF had been landing at St Malo since the 13th of that month. The men of the 52nd (Lowland) Division, largely made up of the 7th/9th Royal Scots and 4th and 5th King's Own Scottish Borderers, made first for Laval and there heard that the Germans had entered Paris. On the 16 June emergency plans were made fro their evacuation from Cherbourg so that the men had to fight a rearguard action along the Cotentin Peninsula before amking their escape from the port. 'We'll be coming back,' shouted a scotsman. 'Ye've no seen the last of my bonnet and me!' The next day, the Germans occupied the town.

ALL-OUT ATTACK ON CHERBOURG

◆

PORT ALMOST ENCIRCLED

INTENSE ARTILLERY AND AIR BOMBARDMENT

ENEMY DESTROYING HARBOUR INSTALLATIONS

An all-out attack against Cherbourg has been launched by the Americans after an intense artillery and air bombardment. On Wednesday night the port had been almost encircled. Last night's official allied report announced that the encirclement of the fortress was almost complete.

Inside the port the Germans, who have been driven back on to the defences in much disorder, are destroying harbour installations and freight trains.

On the eastern sector of the Normandy front the British and Canadians, whose holding of large German forces has aided the American advance in the peninsula, are still engaged in swaying fighting.

ROAD TO CAPE CUT

SWIFT ADVANCE ON COASTS

What is described by war correspondents as an all-out attack on Cherbourg was launched by the American forces under General Bradley at mid-day yesterday. By Wednesday night the encirclement of Cherbourg was almost complete, and, with the Germans withdrawing their troops within the perimeter, without any great show of resistance, the way was clear for the assault.

The position on Wednesday night was that the Americans were across the road leading to St. Pierre Eglise and were in possession of the village ; they cut the road to Cap de la Hague ; and in the centre they pushed their advance to within three miles of the port. The line ran roughly from

INFANTRY PUSHING ON

SHARP COUNTER-ATTACK REPULSED

WITH U.S. FORCES, June 22.—The position at 5.30 this evening in the Cherbourg peninsula—three and a half hours after the attack was launched—is that American troops in their three-pronged drive are making steady progress, in spite of stiffening resistance. A sharp German counter-attack has been repulsed, and American infantry, backed by artillery, are within the four-mile defence perimeter of Cherbourg, and are pushing forward.

For 80 minutes in the opening stage of the attack more than 1,000 American and British bombers flew in wave after wave and dumped tons of explosive on the German fortifications surrounding Cherbourg, and American land forces then forged ahead in an all-out assault on the German fortress harbour.

Fighter-bombers raced in and dived over our heads, dropping their loads in the narrow strip now separating the beleaguered German

TWO FORTS UNDER GUNFIRE

SWEEPING ADVANCE

BATTLE OF ARMOUR IN BRITISH SECTOR

From Our Special Correspondent

H.Q., 21ST ARMY GROUP, JUNE 22

Cherbourg is now almost completely encircled on the landward side by the attacking American forces. There were even reports to-day that the forts at Octeville on the south-western outskirts of the town and Fort du Roule to the south-east of it were under allied gunfire.

North-eastward from Valognes the advance has swept up to St. Pierre Eglise, little more than three miles from the coast, and over to the north-west it extends across the base of the tip of land which finishes at Cap de la Hague. There seems good reason to believe that the enemy has withdrawn virtually all his forces within the actual defences of Cherbourg.

South of St. Sauveur the front is still quiet, and little is happening also along the line south-west and south of Carentan. Between Tilly and the area north of Caen, however, there is little diminution of the violence which has all along characterized the battle of the British armoured troops and supporting infantry against the very heavy enemy armour. In this desperate fight our men have made no great gains or suffered any great losses in territory, but they are doing priceless service by keeping away from the Cotentin peninsula German tank formations which could be a factor of considerable embarrassment to the Americans attacking Cherbourg. When the port falls they must be remembered as having had their share in a great allied achievement.

The weather improved yesterday and to-day, but is still far from favourable to our unloading work at the beaches. The trouble is in the prevailing wind which blows on to the French coast.

ENEMY DIVISIONS' DISORDER

DEMOLITIONS IN HARBOUR

FROM OUR SPECIAL CORRESPONDENT

CHERBOURG FRONT, JUNE 21
(Delayed)

Inside the port of Cherbourg the Germans are already reported to be destroying harbour installations and freight trains, but the hacked divisions driven back on to the perimeter defences are in considerable disorder, as is suggested by the capture intact of tanks and guns.

For the most part the divisions are second-rate troops drawn from all over occupied Europe, who fight only because their officers and n.c.o.s shoot them if they attempt to come over. Many of the better class German troops succeeded in breaking out to the south before the net closed, but nevertheless it would be the wish of the High Command to hold

The Times of Friday 23 June describes the beginning of the assault on Cherbourg. The town fell to the Americans two days later.

After D-Day in June 1944, the capture of the town was essential in order to ensure the supply of war materials to the Allied armies. By the 22 June, the US 4th, 9th and 79th Divisions were in a position to begin a co-ordinated assault on the port. After heavy air attacks, the Americans took the airfield at Mauperthius and, on 24 June, entered the outskirts of the town. Hitler instructed General von Schlieben, the German commander, 'it is our duty to defend the last bunker and leave to the enemy not a harbour but a field of ruins'. The town was well fortified with concrete bunkers and, high on a rocky promontory above the town, stood the formidable Bastion, the Fort du Roule, with its nests of machine-guns running across its rock-face. After savage fighting, the fort fell to the Americans on 25 June. On that day too, the Germans holding the centre of the town capitulated and then, on 27 June, the sailors defending the thick-walled naval arsenal also surrendered. Even so, there were still die-hard fanatics determined to make a last stand on the fortifications of the outer harbour and breakwater. They resisted for a further two days before the struggle for Cherbourg was finally over.

The Americans found the port mined and blocked with sunken ships and the harbour buildings totally devastated. Engineers and frogmen worked to make the port operational again. After three weeks it was able to receive its first ships but it was several months before it was working to full capacity.

On 12 August, 'PLUTO' (Pipe Line Under The Ocean), a submarine pipe-line carrying much-needed fuel, began to operate between the Isle of Wight and Cherbourg.

Today, the Fort du Roule still stands guard over the town and visitors can climb to it along a steep, winding road. Its main building is now a museum. In the entrance is a mural depicting the defence and capture of the fort and its map room contains twenty relief maps giving an overall picture of the Normandy campaign and the events leading to the end of the war. The armoury contains a collection of uniforms and equipment. Along the harbour and breakwater, the German concrete bunkers remain. On the hill just off the *Route des Pieux* leading up to Octeville is the town's cemetery and part of it contains British war graves. In it lie the men of the Second BEF who fell in 1940 as they tried to make good their escape from Cherbourg and the crews of several RAF aircraft that crashed in the vicinity during the course of the war. These include the pilots of a Hurricane and a Spitfire (Group Captain Hope and Sergeant Jacka) who were both shot down in August 1941, the crews of a Wellington bomber (piloted by Sergeant J.H. Wilcox) shot down in October 1942, of a Polish-manned Wellington shot down in January 1943, the crew of another Wellington (piloted by Flight Sergeant Hennessey) shot down as it returned from dropping leaflets over Paris in June 1943 and of an RAF Mitchell bomber (piloted by an American, Flying Officer Solheim) which was shot down over Martinvast in November 1943. Nearby is a French military cemetery and the graves of the many citizens of Cherbourg who died during the liberation of their town. Interestingly the same cemetery contains the graves of the sailors who perished during the 'Alabama incident'. On 19 June 1864, during the American Civil War, the Yankee sloop *Kearsarge* fought an engagement with the Confederate cruiser *Alabama* off the coast at the tip of the Cotentin Peninsula. The *Alabama*, which had been built in Britain and then sold to the Confederacy, had wrought havoc among Federal shipping and this had led to strained relations between Britain and the North. The British government subsequently agreed to pay $15,500,000 compensation in respect of the damage done by the *Alabama*.

▶ COLLEVILLE-MONTGOMERY

Colleville-Montgomery, or just plain Colleville as the community was originally known, lies a short distance to the west of Ouistreham and four kilometres inland from the coastal resort Colleville-Montgomery Plage. To reach the small township, either travel along the coast road (D514) to Colleville-Montgomery Plage and then follow the D604 inland or follow the D514 after leaving Ouistreham and after three kilometres turn to the right along the D35 towards St Aubin-d'Arquenay.

On D-Day, Colleville Plage was in the centre of 'Queen' sector of Sword Beach and it is here that the 3rd British Division made its way ashore, led by 1st South Lancashire and 2nd East Yorkshire Regiments, following what has been described as 'the most effective air and warship bombardment on any of the D-Day beaches'. Nearby Hermanville was quickly taken but at Colleville there were difficulties. Behind the beaches and on the outskirts of Colleville, the Germans had built two key strongpoints – 'Morris' and 'Hillman'. After a heavy bombardment, the Germans defending 'Morris' surrendered but 'Hillman' proved a far more difficult proposition. The strongpoint, which was garrisoned by 150 men equipped with machine-guns and anti-tank guns, consisted of twelve emplacements with concrete up to three-and-a-half metres thick. After a tank with a 75mm gun had failed to make any impression on the bunkers there was some delay before the 1st Suffolk Regiment, supported by tanks of the Royal Hussars and Staffordshire Yeomanry, moved forward. In spite of the barbed wire and raking machine-gun fire from the German positions, the Suffolks used explosives to blow open the bunkers and finally succeeded in storming the strongpoint.

After the war, Colleville honoured the commander-in-chief of the Allied land forces by changing its name to Colleville-Montgomery. To reach the former German strongpoint, 'Hillman', follow the *Rue du Suffolk Regiment* from the centre of the village to the top of the hill. What remains of 'Morris' is on private ground and most of the bunkers have been adapted for farming purposes.

COLEVILLE-MONTGOMERY PLAGE

Back on the coast at Colleville-Montgomery Plage there are two interesting memorials on each side of the road leading to the beach. Erected on 6 June 1945, one commemorates *'des premiers Alliés tombés le 6 juin 1944'* and the arrival on the beach of the troops of General Montgomery and French Commando leader, Captain Kieffer. It also records the decision of the town to change its name to Colleville-Montgomery so that future generations would remember *'les exploits de ces héros sublime, personnifiés par un chef valeureux'*. The memorial opposite is also to Captain Kieffer.

🐾 COLLEVILLE-SUR-MER

Colleville-sur-Mer (not to be confused with Colleville-Montgomery) is an extended village which runs along the D514 immediately behind Omaha Beach and is just three kilometres to the east of St Laurent.

On D-Day, it was just to the north of the village that the Americans came so close to the brink of disaster on Omaha Beach, but today no evidence remains of those hectic days of June 1944. In the village churchyard lies the grave of a twenty-one-year-old RAF pilot, Sergeant Hector Barrow of Isleworth, Middlesex. The sergeant, who flew a Hurricane of 213 Squadron, was killed on 28 November 1940.

Before the church, turn to the right and follow the road towards Plage de Colleville-sur-Mer. Halfway along, turn to the left along a one-way road which leads uphill to the American Military Cemetery. Close to the top there is a car park from which it is possible to walk to visit two memorials. One is dedicated to the 5th Engineer Special Brigade and the other, obelisk-shaped and surrounded by seats, is to the US First Infantry Division. (Both these monuments can also be reached directly from the American Military Cemetery and Memorial.)

🐾 COURSEULLES-SUR-MER

Famous as a fishing port and for its oyster-beds, the rapidly expanding Courseulles-sur-Mer lies at the mouth of the River Seulles. It is situated roughly half-way between Arromanches-les-Bains and Ouistreham. It can be reached by following the coast road (N514) to where the town is squeezed between its coastal neighbours, Graye-sur-Mer and Bernières-sur-Mer.

On D-Day, the town lay in the centre of Juno Beach and it was here that the Canadian 7th Infantry Brigade came ashore led by Regina Rifles and the 1st Canadian Scottish Regiment. Because of problems caused by prevailing tides and off-shore rocks, the landing time had to be delayed for fifteen minutes and when they reached the beach the Canadians faced a quite daunting task. The town was particularly well-fortified and, with few of their supporting tanks making it ashore, there was a prolonged period of fierce street fighting before the town was finally liberated late in the afternoon.

Entering the town from Graye-sur-Mer and still on the west bank of the river, the dunes are dominated by a quite massive Cross of Lorraine. Visible from a distance, the monument celebrates General de Gaulle's return to France in June 1944. Along the usually busy seafront on the east bank of the river is a Sherman tank. Named 'Bold', it originally belonged to the 6th Canadian Armoured Regiment (First Hussars). During 1970, the tank was recovered from three miles out to sea and, once restored, placed on its present site – a memorial dedicated to its former regiment. Nearby is a monument which records the fact that General de Gaulle landed there on 14 June on his way to Bayeux. Two days earlier the town had been visited by Winston Churchill and two days later it was visited by King George VI. Each side of the steps leading to the beach there are memorials – one to the Regina Rifle Regiment and the other to the 1st Canadian Scottish Regiment and the *Federationem Voluntarii Belgae*. To the east of the town and a short walk along the promenade is a large dagger-shaped memorial to the Royal Winnipeg Rifles, the 'Little Black Devils'. It was erected to mark the twentieth anniversary of D-Day, in June 1964.

In *Nothing Less Than Victory: The Oral History of D-Day* by Russell Miller there is a gripping account by Sergeant Leo Gariepy, 6th Canadian Armoured Regiment, of the hazards of swimming tanks. Here is a taster:

Suddenly, at 7,000 yards, our squadron commander, Major Duncan, asked if we would prefer to risk it. Cheers went up, we were all for it, and the CO, knowing very well what we were facing, agreed and we prepared to launch. The LCT once again took its launching position in the wind, the ramp was lowered and we each, in turn, rolled off. The manoeuvre was difficult owing to the wind and waves. DD tanks had been conceived for a Force 4 wind and we were operating in about a Force 7.

All our five tanks were successfully launched and we ploughed into the water, trying to adopt a pre-determined attack formation. (We couldn't fire our guns in the water, because they were hidden behind the huge canvas screen which kept us afloat.) Standing on the command deck at the back of my turret, trying to steer and navigate, that 7,000 yards to the beach was the longest journey of my life.

Enemy fire was discernable now. Machine-gun bullets were ripping the water all around me and an occasional mortar shell fell among us. I looked behind to see how the others were faring and noticed that many of the tanks had sunk and the crews were desperately trying to board bright-yellow salvage dinghies.

🐾 CREULLY

The township of Creully lies fourteen kilometres to the east of Bayeux (on theD12), ten kilometres south of Arromanches-les-Bains (on the D65) and eighteen kilometres from Caen (on the D22).

On D-Day, the 4th/7th Royal Dragoon Guards, who had earlier landed on Gold Beach, passed through its streets without opposition. The picturesque town, which overlooks the Seulles valley, achieved fame later in the month when General Montgomery set up his caravan headquarters in the grounds of the nearby fifteenth-century Château Creullet.

Approaching the town on the D6S you first pass the Château Creullet, which is on the right-hand-side, in its own grounds and set back from the road. Then, a little further on the left-hand-side just before entering the town, you pass an impressive memorial to the 4th/7th Royal Dragoon Guards. The inscription on the memorial reads:

> In proud memory
> of the 4th/7th Royal Dragoon Guards
> who lived or died in the fight for freedom
> landing in France September 1939
> withdrawing through Dunkirk June 1940
> returning to Normandy to assault King Beach
> La Rivière at H Hour on D Day 6th June 1944
> to liberate Creully later that day
> and in due course to assist in bringing the fight
> to a successful conclusion
> *Quis separabit*

Inside the *mairie*, which is situated in the town's square, is a Royal Engineers commemorative stone and a plaque which reads, 'During the critical days of June and July 1944, the world listened to news of the Battle of Normandy, broadcast by radio correspondents of many nations from the BBC studio in the centre of this castle'.

🐗 CRICQUEVILLE-EN-BESSIN

The small hamlet of Cricqueville-en-Bessin lies midway between Vierville-sur-Mer and Grandcamp-Maisy and is close to the Pointe du Hoc. Travelling west, leave the D514 just before you reach Grandcamp-Maisy and follow the narrow D194 to the village.

Americans moving inland from Omaha Beach reached Cricqueville-en-Bessin on the 8 June as they advanced westward towards La Cambe and Isigny-sur-Mer.

The village church contains a memorial to the American Rangers (the church is usually locked but the key can be obtained at the *mairie*). Outside there is an unusual memorial to local men who fell in the Great War, 1914-18, and to this has been added a plaque listing the names of the civilian victims of June 1944.

CRISBECQ

The German battery at Crisbecq lies close to St Marcouf de l'Isle to the north-west of the main American landing areas along Utah Beach. Drive northwards along the coast road (D421) to Ravenoville Plage and shortly afterwards, at Les Gaugins, turn left along the D69 and follow the narrow road for three kilometres. Parking is available at the site of the battery.

The concrete gun positions and bunkers at Crisbecq were part of the Atlantic Wall fortifications intended to defend the east coast of the Cotentin Peninsula. Built by the slave labourers of the Todt organisation, the battery was manned by three hundred men and bristled with machine-gun posts and anti-aircraft guns. Its two large 155mm guns were ranged on the nearby beaches. Before dawn on D-Day, heavy bombing failed to knock out the battery and, at daybreak, its guns were able to sink a destroyer and damage a cruiser and several other ships. Even when the battery's guns were silenced, the Germans under their young commanding officer, Walter Ohmsen, continued to fight bravely and held out for a further six days. On 12 June, men of the American 39th Infantry Regiment finally overran the German positions.

Although dynamited by American engineers after their capture, the bunkers and casemates remain largely intact. From the top of a viewing platform it is possible to get a panoramic view of the coastline towards Utah Beach. Some of the gun emplacements are across the road and on private land.

DOUVRES-LA-DÉLIVRANDE

Douvres-la-Délivrande and the adjacent La Délivrande lie inland immediately to the south of Langrune-sur-Mer. They can be reached by leaving the coast road (D514) at Langrune-sur-Mer and then following the D7 for two kilometres. Alternatively, if travelling from Caen, they are sixteen kilometres along the main road leading north out of the city (D7).

On D-Day, Douvres-la-Délivrande lay on the dividing line between Juno and Sword Beaches and was particularly important since it was the site of a well-defended German radar station. Early attempts to take the positions failed and, in spite of several hard-pressed assaults by the 51st Highland Division, the defenders of the station did not surrender until they were finally overwhelmed on 17 June by 41st RM Commando, aided by flail and flame-throwing Churchill tanks of the 22nd Dragoons. The Germans had held their positions for eleven days.

Today, some of the concrete blockhouses of the former radar station complex can still be seen on the outskirts of the town. They are on privately owned agricultural land and the presence of a bull helps to dissuade visitors!

LA DÉLIVRANDE WAR CEMETERY

La Délivrande War Cemetery is on the left-hand side of the road (D7) as you leave the town in the direction of Caen. It is close to the town's three-spired church. The cemetery, set in a picturesque, wooded area, contains 1,123 graves, of which 927 are British and 180 German. Many date from D-Day but some were brought in later from the battlefields between the coast and Caen.

Among those buried in the cemetery is the Australian pilot, Squadron Leader William Blessing DSO, DFC, of 105 Squadron, whose Mosquito was shot down during a raid on Caen on 7 July. His aircraft crashed on one of the Normandy beaches and, although he was killed instantly, his navigator survived. There are also the graves of a twenty-seven-year-old Church of Scotland arm chaplain, the Reverend Cameron Carnegie, who was accidentally killed on 16 July while attached to the RASC, as well as of Major David de Symons Barrow (The Queen's Royal Regiment) and Major Peter Wheelock (KSLI), both holders of the Military Cross.

🐾 ESCOVILLE

Escoville lies just to the south of Hérouvillette. After crossing Pegasus Bridge turn to the right along the D224 and then proceed to Ranville and Hérouville. Escoville is a kilometre further along the D37.

On D-Day, the whole of the area along the east bank of the River Orne was the scene of bitter fighting involving the 3rd and 5th Parachute Brigades. The 8th Parachute Battalion landed to the south of Escoville with the aim of destroying the bridges over the River Dives at Bures and Troarn. At Escoville they met fierce opposition and had to by-pass the village. In *Overlord: D-Day and the Battle for Normany,* Max Hastings describes an incident at Escoville:

> Corporal Werner Jortenhaus of 21st Panzer saw four of his company's 10 tanks brewed up in five minutes during the attack on the château at Escoville on the 9th June. Again and again the Mk IVs crawled forward, supporting infantry huddled behind the protection of their hulls as they advanced into the furious British mortar and shellfire. But when the tanks reversed they were often unable to see behind them, and rolled over the injured or sheltering men who lay in their path. A wounded panzergrenadier cried for his mother from no man's land all one night in front of their position.

Today there is a memorial 'To our British liberators' on the green in front of the church. In the churchyard lies on British soldier, twenty-two-year-old Private William Wilkins from Kingswood, Gloucestershire. He served with The Oxfordshire and Buckinghamshire Light Infantry and lost his life on 7 June. Outside the village at the crossroads where D37 is joined by the D37B there is a monument to the 8th Parachute Battalion 'in memory of all ranks of the Battalion who fought and died for freedom'.

🐾 FONTAINE HENRY

Fontaine Henry, which is twinned with Scoriton in Devon, is a picturesque village situated in the Mue Valley. Leave Caen on the D22 and after twenty kilometres turn to the right at Pierrepont along the D141 and the village is a few kilometres ahead. Alternatively, travel inland from Courseulles-sur-Mer along the D170 and the village lies seven kilometres ahead.

The village is best known for its fine château. Built in the fifteenth century by the Harcourt family, it is a splendid example of Renaissance architecture. As you leave the village, you climb a steep hill and pass a church on the left-hand side. A memorial set into the church wall lists the names of six civilians and five Canadian soldiers who were killed during the liberation of the village in June 1944.

🐾 FONTENAY-LE-PESNEL

The village of Fontenay-le-Pesnel lies sixteen kilometres to the west of Caen on the main road (D9) towards Caumont l'Eventé, just after the junction with the D13.

During July there was a great deal of heavy fighting in the area. One of the units involved in the struggle for the high ground, the Butte de Chêne, was the 1/7th Royal Warwickshires. The battalion history recalls:

> Like other units in Normandy, the 1/7th was experiencing an acute shortage of officers ... All through July 30 the crump of enemy mortaring was heard around the position. Though everyone dug in, several more became casualties, and movement of any kind was extremely risky ... Where so few officers were left, the NCOs who were left played an outstanding part. Sergeant A.G. Dix insisted on remaining with his platoon for three days after being hit in the back by mortar-fire. This splendid example of devotion to duty brought him the DCM. Sergeant C. Franks, who won the MM, also commanded a platoon throughout the action with exemplary courage.

FONTENAY-LE-PESNEL WAR CEMETERY

Fontenay-le-Pesnel War Cemetery lies one kilometre south-east of the hamlet of St Martin on the D139 to Grainville-sur-Oden. Look out for the impressive memorial to the

49th (West Riding) Division and a track leading to the cemetery is directly opposite. Here lie 456 British, 4 Canadian and 59 German soldiers who lost their lives during fighting to the west of Caen in June and July 1944. They include many men of The Royal Warwickshires, including Private Kelly, whose parents requested the epitaph, 'Beneath foreign soil our darling son is laid but in our hearts his memory forever is engraved'. The cemetery also contains the graves of many men of the Durham Light Infantry, the East Lancashires and the South Staffordshires.

GONNEVILLE-EN-AUGE

Gonneville-en-Auge is a small hamlet immediately to the south of the former German battery at Merville (see Merville-Franceville Plage).

It was a sad misfortune for the people of Gonneville that on the morning of D-Day their homes were mistaken for the German gun positions at Merville and their village was heavily bombed. Disasters resulting from mistaken identity were not uncommon. On the same day, a number of British paratroopers who had landed some fifteen kilometres from their rendezvous area were strafed by Allied aircraft under orders to 'attack any movement'. In all, some forty men were killed.

In his book *Red Berets into Normandy*, the late Sir Huw Wheldon recalled:

> In the distance they could hear the intermittent sounds of machine-gun fire, while close at hand the groans and bellowings of injured cattle, and fresh bomb craters, bore witness to the bombings of two hours before. Near Gonneville, they froze suddenly, as a patrol of twenty Germans crossed the track twenty-five metres ahead of them and then, with sighs of relief, they continued their advance. A small scouting party had landed in advance of the battalion. At the road junction near the battery, just past Gonneville, the party met the oncoming troops. They reported that the bombing attack had missed the battery.

Today Gonneville-en-Auge remains a small, peaceful hamlet. Only the memorial in the village churchyard records the loss of life suffered by local families on that day.

GRANDCAMP-MAISY

Grandcamp-Maisy lies thirty-one kilometres to the north-west of Bayeux on the D514, midway between Vierville-sur-Mer and Isigny-sur-Mer.

On D-Day, the coastal town was some distance to the west of the main American landings on Omaha Beach but close to the Pointe du Hoc, the promontory stormed by the American Rangers. During the days that followed, the town was largely by-passed as the US 29th Division smashed its way through the German 352 Infantry Division to reach Isigny-sur-Mer on 9 June and then surge westwards towards Carentan.

Just off the D514 at the entrance to the town is an interesting communal cemetery which lies around the ruins of a church destroyed during the fighting in the area. It contains the grave of an RAF pilot, Flying Officer Nicholas Peel, a clergyman's son from Woodborough in Wiltshire. A Spitfire pilot with 140 Squadron, he was shot down on 24 November 1941. Close by lies the popular French hero of the landings on Sword Beach, Commandant Philippe Kieffer. The former leader of French No. 7 and No. 8 Troops of No. 10 Inter-Allied Commando, he was described as 'tall, burly with round blue eyes' and having a 'rolling gait as he walked'. Once returned to French soil as part of the French contingent of No. 4 Commando, Kieffer's dash and bravery became legendary. It was said that his son was killed fighting for the Resistance shortly before his father entered Paris with the Free French Forces.

In the town, there is a small *Musée des Rangers* and a memorial to the Guyenne and *Tunisie* Squadrons of the French Air Force which formed 346 and 347 Squadrons of RAF Bomber Command. Based at Elvington near York, they flew Halifax bombers and transport planes and in one ten-month period jointly took part in nearly three thousand operational sorties. In October 1945, the squadrons were disbanded and their personnel returned home taking with them a number of Halifaxes which had been presented to France by the British government.

🐾 GRAYE-SUR-MER

Graye-sur-Mer lies immediately to the west of Courseulles-sur-Mer and might be considered an extension of that town. On the D514, the village is eighteen kilometres from Arromanches-les-Bains and just over twenty kilometres from Ouistreham.

On D-Day, Graye-sur-Mer was on the edge of Mike sector of Juno Beach. Like most of the coastline, the beach was protected with barbed wire, mines and concrete pillboxes and bunkers. At 7.45 a.m., Canadians of the Royal Winnipeg Rifles and 6th Armoured Regiment came ashore accompanied by units of the 26th Assault Squadron of the Royal Engineers. The problem was that an exit from the beach was blocked by an anti-tank ditch and a flooded culvert which was connected to the River Seulles. One Churchill AVRE tank went forward and filled the tank trap with a fascine (a two-ton bundle of logs). A second tank advanced to the culvert but misjudged its size and, before it could drop its fascine, it began to slide slowly under the water. Several of the crew were killed as they made their escape. Afterwards, the tank was allowed to remain in the culvert where, with additional rubble, it became part of the exit road. Later it was all concreted over.

Today there is a Comité du Débarquement memorial on the dunes at Graye-sur-Mer and near it a Churchill tank. This is 'One Charlie', the tank left in the culvert in 1944. It was recovered in 1976 and, after renovation, placed on the beach as a memorial. George Dunn, the tank's original driver, was present at the inauguration ceremony. Elsewhere along the coast lie the remains of numerous German bunkers.

HERMANVILLE-SUR-MER

The village of Hermanville-sur-Mer lies a short distance inland to the south of Lion-sur-Mer and La Brêche d'Hermanville. It is reached by leaving the D514 in Lion-sur-Mer and following the D60 for three kilometres. Alternatively, if travelling from Caen, it is thirteen kilometres distant along the D60.

On 6 June 1944, the village lay behind Sword Beach and was liberated by units of the British 3rd Army advancing inland from the coast. The 1st South Lancashires and the 2nd King's Own Shropshire Light Infantry entered the village at 9 a.m. 'They marched down the road into Hermanville amid the cheers of excited local civilians, and the encouraging spectacle of clusters of German prisoners being herded in the opposite direction'. Then, together with other units of 185 Brigade, they assembled in readiness to advance on Caen.

In the village is the well of 'Mare Saint Pierre', which supplied the British forces with one-and-a-half million gallons of water between 6 June and 1 July. There is also a memorial which recalls the names of the five merchant ships scuttled off the coast at Hermanville in order to create an artificial harbour during the period 6 to 9 June.

HERMANVILLE WAR CEMETERY

Hermanville War Cemetery is to the north of the village. Pass the *mairie*, which is on your left, and then turn right and continue for a further three hundred metres. The cemetery is then approached along a path.

All but nineteen of the 1,005 buried there are British and were killed either on D-Day or during the early stages of the advance on Caen. Among the interesting graves is that of Private K.W. Graham of the Hampshire Regiment who served with No. 10 (Inter-Allied) Commando.

This unit was made up of men of other nations – French, Belgian, Dutch, Swedish, Danish and Norwegian and a number of German Jews. The Jews could only expect the harshest of treatment if they were taken prisoner and were provided with false names, papers and identity discs. Twenty-four-year-old Private Kenneth Graham's real name was Kurt Gumpertz and he was killed on the 12 June. Also buried in the cemetery are the Roman Catholic padre, the Reverend Peter Firth, who came from Scorton in Lancashire and fell on 7 June, and the Reverend Henry Wagg, an Anglican curate from

Lancing in Sussex, who was attached to the 11th Armoured Division. He was killed in action on 18 July 1944. Three adjoining headstones mark the graves of eight drivers of the Royal Army Service Corps who all lost their lives on 8 June 1944.

LA BRÊCHE D'HERMANVILLE

On the coast and situated immediately next to Colleville-Montgomery Plage on the D514 is La Brêche d'Hermanville.

Like its neighbour, on D-Day it shared a central position in the 'Queen' section of Sword Beach. Close to the seafront and set in a square there are a Churchill AVRE tank and two other memorials. In a central position there is a memorial to '*Les Pionniers Alliés*' – the men who manned two midget submarines that were used as markers on D-Day – and to the right a stone which commemorates 'the headquarters and five regiments of the Royal Artillery in the British 3rd Infantry Division which, after firing their guns from the sea, landed on 6th June 1944 and continued firing from the beaches and fields around Hermanville.'

🐦 HÉROUVILLETTE

On the east bank of the River Orne and less than two kilometres south-east of Ranville is the village of Hérouvillette. Once across Pegasus Bridge, take the second turning on the right to Ranville (D37) and continue on to Hérouvillette.

The village was liberated by the 2nd Oxfordshire and Buckinghamshire Light Infantry and 1st Royal Ulster Rifles on the 7 June. The story is told in the Regimental War Diary:

> 7th June. At 04.30 hrs on the 7th June the Regiment moved off towards Hérouvillette. C Company, in the lead, soon reported Hérouvillette clear of the enemy, the handful of the enemy there having run off in the direction of Escoville. At Hérouvillette, we rescued an injured glider pilot who had been locked up in an attic without food and water for twenty-four hours.

Forty-eight hours later the defenders repulsed an attempt by the German 21st Panzer Division to retake the village.

> 9th June. At approximately 18.30 hrs the enemy opened his attack with heavy concentrations of mortar and artillery fire. Messerschmitt 109 aircraft carried out a series of strafing attacks on the village of Hérouvillette. This softening-up process was followed by an attack ... carried out by tanks, self-propelled guns and infantry. The enemy got to within a hundred

yards of the forward Regimental positions held by C and D Companies, but in face of intense fire could advance no further. At about 21.30 hrs he withdrew ...

In the village, take the turning to the left after the church, the *Rue de la Libération*. A little way along is the communal cemetery which contains the graves of twenty-seven soldiers of the 12th Parachute Battalion and the Oxfordshire and Buckinghamshire Light Infantry. Their headstones form a line along the far wall. Three of the paratroopers were only nineteen years old – Private Robert Leadbetter from Glasgow, Private Munro Meiklejohn from Brighton and Private David O'Sullivan from Cwmbran in Gwent. Outside on the wall there is a memorial to the 2nd (Airborne) Bn The Oxfordshire and Buckinghamshire LI (52nd), 'In memory of those who fought at Pegasus Bridge, Escoville, Hérouvillette, Bréville-les-Monts and to the Seine and of the many brave French who helped us'.

HILL 112 – 'CORNWALL HILL'

Hill 112 lies some eight kilometres to the south-west of Caen. It can be reached by following the D8 out of the city on the road to Evrecy. Travel three kilometres beyond Eterville to where the road forks (D8/D36) and Hill 112 appears on the left-hand side. It is more a gradual slope than a hill and is not easily identifiable.

In the battle for Caen, Hill 112, with its commanding position beyond the River Odon, was the scene of some of the most ferocious fighting of the whole Normandy campaign. The Germans believed that 'he who holds Hill 112 holds Normandy' and time and time again ground was taken by one side and then the other only to be lost to a counter-attack. In two days' fighting, 10-11 July, the 43rd (Wessex) Division suffered two thousand casualties when it took on battle hardened SS Panzers and some of the best German infantry units fighting in Normandy. The Hill was not finally cleared of the enemy until 3 August – 'dawn broke with an eerie silence and heavy scent of death. Stubble-chinned, dirty, dust–covered infantrymen emerged from holes in the ground.' The capture of Hill 112 was the prelude to the final Allied victory in Normandy.

> Yet there is nothing spectacular about Hill 112. It rises gently from the valley of the Odon river, which is itself little more than a stream. The tourist in his fast car travelling west out of Caen along the Route Nationale Nr 175 would find it difficult to believe that he was driving through what was known as 'Death Valley'. It was the stretch of road which saw the heaviest bombardment of the Normandy campaign. And that rounded dome of green countryside south of the road! Is that Hill 112? It scarcely warrants a second glance.
>
> *From:* Hill 112 *by Major J. J. How, M.C.*

In the struggle for Hill 112, the 5th Duke of Cornwall's Light Infantry suffered 320 casualties of whom only one was taken prisoner. Immediately after the battle, ninety-three who fell were buried on the Hill. Not surprisingly, the Hill has come to be known as 'Cornwall Hill'.

Today, the same *calvaire*, or crucifix calvary, which was there at the time of the battle still stands at the edge of the road and by it there is now a granite monument dedicated to all ranks of the 43rd (Wessex) Division. There is a lane which can be followed across fields to the crest of the hill. The wood, where so many men died, was known to soldiers as the 'Crown of thorns'. Today it is not accessible to the public. Like the old Somme battlefield of the Great War, it remains a place where rusting shrapnel can still quite easily be found in newly ploughed fields.

🔫 HOTTOT-LES-BAGUES

Hottot-les-Bagues is to the south-east of Bayeux. Follow the D6 for twelve kilometres to Tilly-sur-Seulles and then continue to Juvigny-sur-Seulles where the road joins the D9 from Caen to Caumont L'Éventé.

It was the 1st Hampshire Regiment that first reached the village on the 19 June. Their Regimental History records:

> The attack on Hottot started in pouring rain which began before noon. The start line was marked with white tape and the enemy gave it (and us) a terrific plastering with his mortars. We pushed forward under a heavy barrage with our Brens fighting a staccato duel against the b-r-r-r-p of Jerry's Spandaus.

In fact, the Hampshires were up against the crack German Panzer Lehr Division. Made up of veterans and superbly equipped, it was described as 'the finest armoured division in the *Wehrmacht*'. Hottot-les-Bagues fell three weeks later after a period of incessant fighting.

HOTTOT-LES-BAGUES WAR CEMETARY

To reach Hottot-les-Bagues War Cemetary turn right along the D9 towards Caumont L'Éventé and it is just a few hundred metres on the right-hand side of the road. The cemetery contains 1,137 burials of which 965 are British and 132 German. The men buried there were killed during the heavy fighting to the west of Caen during June and early July 1944.

🪖 ISIGNY-SUR-MER

At the south of the Contenin Peninsula and close to the border between the regions of Manche and Calvados, Isigny-sur-Mer lies on the estuary of the River Vire. Eleven kilometres to the east of Carentan and thirty-one kilometres to the west of Bayeux, the centre, long famous for its dairy produce, is now by-passed by the N13.

An intended objective on D-Day of the US 29th Infantry Division under Brigadier-General Norman Cota, the hold-up on Omaha Beach meant that the town was not taken as planned. On the night of 8/9 June, Isigny-sur-Mer was subjected to a naval bombardment which destroyed 60 per cent of its buildings. In fact, it was all quite needless since the following morning the town was liberated without a fight. By 12 June, the road west from Isigny to Carentan had also been cleared of the enemy.

Today, the town centre is usually very busy. There is a *Comité du Débarquement* monument which marks the spot where on the 14 June 1944 General de Gaulle stood and 'spoke to the French people freed by the Allied forces'. While in the centre of an area famous for its dairy produce, you might like to join in one of the conducted tours of a local creamery. It is best to book in advance.

🪖 JERUSALEM WAR CEMETERY, CHOUAIN

From Bayeux take the D6 and follow the road south-east towards Tilly-sur-Seulles. Jerusalem War Cemetery will be found after about eight kilometres on the left-hand side of the road at the bottom of a downhill stretch.

Named after a tiny hamlet close to the nearby village of Chouain and with only forty-seven burials, it is the smallest British cemetery of the Second World War to be found in Normandy. The cemetery was begun on 10 June and half the men buried there served with the Durham Light Infantry. Of interest is the fact that two army chaplains, one Anglican and the other Roman Catholic, lie side by side. One, the Reverend Cecil Hawkesworth, curate of Saint Peter's, Croydon, had already served in the Sudan, Eritrea and with the 8th Army in North Africa. In 1944, he was attached to the 6th Durham Light Infantry and was killed as a result of an accident on 7 July. The other, the Reverend G. Nesbitt, had also served with the 8th Army in North Africa. Attached to the 8th Durham Light Infantry, he was killed in action on 5 July.

🪖 LA CAMBE

The village of La Cambe lies on the N13, the main Bayeux-Cherbourg road and is some nineteen kilometres to the east of Carentan.

Above left: Private Emile Cortell and his dog Glen, who were both killed on D-Day.

Above right: Private Cortell's grave.

Right: The grave of sixteen-year-old paratrooper Robert Johns.

Above: The church and square at St Mère-Église today.

Left: John Steele. The ex-paratrooper was a regular visitor to St Mère-Église until his death in 1969.

Maurice Duboscq – Papa
Maurice, the railway-crossing
attendant.

The grave of Papa Maurice and
his son, Claude, in the village
cemetery.

The American Military Cemetery above Omaha beach. The cemetery contains the graves of 9,386 US servicemen.

The Utah Beach Museum, built on a former German strongpoint along the Plage de la Madeleine.

A Sherman tank at the Utah Beach Museum.

Above: The monument to the 2nd Ranger Battalion at Pointe du Hoc.

Left: The Pegasus Bridge sign with the canal bridge in the background.

Above: The café of Georges and Thérèse Gondrée close to the canal bridge.

Right: The memorial next to the bridge over the River Orne-Horsa Bridge.

"HORSA" BRIDGE

SOON AFTER MIDNIGHT ON 5/6 JUNE 1944, A HORSA GLIDER, FLOWN BY S/SGTS R A HOWARD AND F W BAACKE, GLIDER PILOT REGIMENT, LANDED NORTH WEST OF THIS BRIDGE WITH A PLATOON OF OXF. & BUCKS LIGHT INFANTRY LED BY Lt D FOX AND ROYAL ENGINEERS UNDER Lt J BENCE. THEY CAPTURED THE BRIDGE. A SECOND PLATOON UNDER Lt H J SWEENEY LANDED NEAR BY PILOTED BY S/SGTS S PEARSON AND L GUTHRIE, AND REINFORCED THEM

TRES TOT LE MATIN DU JOUR J, UN PLANEUR HORSA PILOTE PAR R HOWARD ET F BAACKE DU REGIMENT DES PILOTES DE PLANEURS ATTERRIT PRES DE CE PONT, AVEC DES SOLDATS DU 52e REGIMENT D'INFANTERIE SOUS LE COMMANDEMENT DU Lt FOX, ET AVEC DES SAPEURS DU GENIE ROYAL SOUS LES ORDRES DU Lt BENCE. ILS SAISIRENT LE PONT. UN DEUXIEME PELOTON AVEC LE Lt H SWEENEY SUIVIT DANS UN PLANEUR PILOTE PAR S PEARSON ET L GUTHRIE, ET LES RENFORCA.

Left: A memorial to the 'Canadian Liberators' at Basly.

Right: A window in the church at St Mère-Église commemorating the liberation of the town by American paratroopers, 6 June 1944.

Below: The British War Cemetery at Hermanville.

Just to the west of the village and at the side of the road is a large German war cemetery. To begin with, the cemetery was used for the burial of both American and German servicemen. In 1947, the Americans arranged to have the bodies of their dead either returned to the United States or reinterred in the large cemetery at St Laurent which overlooks Omaha Beach. Afterwards the German dead, many of whom had been previously buried in a number of cemeteries spread across the region, were brought together at La Cambe. The cemetery was completed in September 1961 and is now administered by the *Deutsche Kriegsgräberfürsorge*, the Gemian equivalent of the Commonwealth War Graves Commission. The entrance to the cemetery has a room on either side. One is a chapel of remembrance and the other contains registers, a visitors' book and other literature. The cemetery itself is the resting place of 21,160 German dead. Unlike British headstones, German stones are grey crosses placed flat on the ground. Each is engraved with three, four or more names. Interdispersed across the cemetery are groups of five stone crosses. In the centre is a grassed mound surmounted by a cross and two engraved figures which represent grieving parents. The mound is the mass grave of 296 men whose names are listed on a series of stone tablets at the base.

🪖 LANGRUNE-SUR-MER

Langrune-sur-Mer, a sea-front continuation of St Aubin-sur-Mer, is eleven kilometres from Ouistreham (D514) or can be reached directly from Caen along the D7 (sixteen kilometres).

On 6 June, Langrune-sur-Mer was virtually at the point where Juno Beach, the landing area of the 3rd Canadian Division, joined with Sword Beach, the area allocated to the 3rd British Division. No landing was made here on D-Day since it was the intention that 48 Royal Marine Commando, advancing from the west, would link up to the south with 41 Royal Marine Commando, which had landed to the east at Lion-sur-Mer. Stiff German resistance prevented this from happening immediately and, as D-Day progressed, the gap between the two beachheads developed into a weakness which the German 21st Panzer Division attempted to exploit. After a concentrated naval bombardment, the heavily fortified town was finally taken on 7 June by British Commandos advancing from St Aubin.

On the sea-front at Langrune-sur-Mer is a tablet memorial to 48 Royal Marine Commando.

🪖 LE MESNIL PATRY

Leave the N13 at Bretteville-l'Orgueilleuse, eleven kilometres to the west of Caen, and follow first the D83 and then the D172 to reach the village of Le Mesnil Patry.

The village was on the edge of the battles around Tilly-sur-Seulles and was the scene of particularly heavy fighting on 11 June.

In the village is an impressive memorial with panels in English and French to 'those gallant Canadians of The Queen's Own Rifles of Canada and The First Hussars of Canada who paid the supreme sacrifice in the ferocious Battle of Le Mesnil Patry – June 11th 1944. We will remember them.'

🎖 LION-SUR-MER

Lion-sur-Mer lies on the coast six kilometres west along the D514 from Ouistreham/Riva Bella. From Caen, it can be reached along the D60 and is three kilometres north of Hermanville-sur-Mer.

On D-Day, the sea-front of the town was on the edge of Queen sector, Sword Beach. At 8.45 a.m., 41 Royal Marine Commando were the first ashore followed by men of the 1st Battalion of the South Lancashire Regiment. Possession of the coastal resort was fiercely contested by the Germans who inflicted heavy casualties on the commandos. The Germans saw this area where Juno and Sword Beaches met as a weakness which might be exploited. In spite of air and naval bombardment, 736 Infantry Regiment held on but were finally forced to yield the town the next day.

Just off the front there are two squares – *the Place du 18 Juin 1940* – which recalls General de Gaulle's famous call to the French people from London on that day, and another which commemorates the landing of the British commandos, the *Place du 41 Royal Marine Commando*. On the edge of the beach there is an unusual memorial, a plaque supported by two pillars, *'aux soldats alliés et aux victimes civiles tombés pour notre liberté'*.

🎖 LONGUES-SUR-MER

Travel west from Arromanches-les-Bains on the D514 and just beyond Manvieux lies the village of Longues-sur-Mer. In the village turn right and follow the signpost to the Batteries de Longues.

The construction of the German naval battery with its four gun positions, searchlights and anti-aircraft guns, began in 1943. By June 1944, it was an important bastion of the Atlantic Wall and presented a threat to any approaching invasion fleet. In spite of previous heavy bombing, the guns of the Longues battery came immediately into action on the morning of D-Day. Blasted by accurate bombardments from HMS *Ajax* and HMS *Argonaut*, the battery was silenced by 8.45 a.m. Later in the day, it resumed firing until it was once again silenced, this time by the guns of the French cruiser *Georges Leygues*. The next day, the garrison finally surrendered to British troops advancing from Arromanches-les-Bains.

BATTERIES DE LONGUES

Today, the coastal battery is a popular tourist attraction. Follow the lane towards the coast and it is possible to park close to the bunkers. They are well preserved and, unlike the batteries at Merville and Crisbecq, some of the guns remain intact and are still on their revolving turntables. A short distance away at the cliff's edge is the battery's observation post which can be entered. From there it is possible to enjoy a panoramic view of what was the western edge of Gold Beach. Imagine the sight the German observers might have witnessed when they looked out to sea on the morning of D-Day!

🦅 LUC-SUR-MER

Another of the resorts along the Côte de Nacre, Luc-sur-Mer lies on the coast (D514) between Langrune-sur-Mer and Lion-sur-Mer. It is eleven kilometres from Ouistreham (D514), eighteen from Caen (D7) and thirty-three from Bayeux (via Arromanches-les-Bains).

Even before D-Day, Luc-sur-Mer had been the site of the first British commando raid in Normandy when, on the night of 27 September 1941, 5th Troop of No. 1 Commando carried out a raid along the coast there. On 6 June 1944, Luc-sur-Mer lay at the western edge of Sword Beach.

There was no direct landing on the beaches there and the town fell to 46 Royal Marine Commando on the morning of the following day.

Above the sea-front is a memorial which recalls both the commando raid of September 1941 and the liberation of the town in June 1944. In the village churchyard are the graves of three British servicemen. They are a twenty-four-year-old RAF pilot, Squadron Leader James Pitcairn Hill DSO, DFC who flew with 83 Squadron and was shot down in September 1940 and two Welshmen, Royal Welch Fusilier Elwyn Edwards and Corporal L. Evans from Ebbw Vale of the South Wales Borderers. Both men lost their lives during the raid in September 1941 while they were serving with No. 1 Commando.

🦅 MERVILLE-FRANCEVILLE

On the east bank of the River Orne, along the N814 just beyond Sallenelles, is the resort of Merville-Franceville. The Merville Battery is well signposted and lies on a hill close to the village.

Set high above the coast and ranged over the Orne estuary and Sword Beach, the destruction of the guns of the Merville battery was one of the vital objectives of British paratroopers early on the morning of D-Day. In order to neutralise the four guns set in heavily defended concrete casemates, airborne landings were to be made by the 9th Battalion of the British Airborne Division and 591 Parachute Squadron, Royal Engineers, under the command of twenty-nine-year-old Colonel Terence Otway of the Royal Ulster Rifles. It was agreed that if the raid was unsuccessful, the Royal Navy would begin a bombardment of Merville battery at 5.15 a.m.

The episode began with a series of disasters. Soon after midnight, RAF Lancaster bombers mistook the nearby village of Gonneville for the battery and completely destroyed the homes of the community with their four thousand-pound bombs. Then the paratroopers themselves were dropped too widely – over fifteen thousand hectares instead of 250 – and some two hundred men simply vanished without trace. They were almost certainly drowned. Finally, the gliders carrying the heavy assault equipment broke their tow-ropes and disappeared into the waters of the English Channel. By 2.30 a.m., only 150 men had reached the assembly point to begin to a way through the minefields and wire. At 4.30 a.m., the gliders with the assault sections arrived but they too landed some distance away. With time getting short, an attack was launched on the battery and there was bitter hand-to-hand fighting between the young British paratroopers and the German gunners. The Merville Battery was under the command of 2/Lt Raimund Steiner. From a respected Innsbruck family, there was some irony in the fact that his father, known to be anti-Nazi, was to die of ill-treatment in a concentration camp! On the morning of the 7 June, with the position still uncertain, the German positions were again attacked by two troops of No. 3 British Commando under the command of Major John Pooley. The fighting was ferocious and the losses on both sides were heavy. The Major himself was among the dead. The battery was finally silenced by the RAF and the guns of the Royal Navy. Once out of action, it was discovered that the guns were only 75mm with a maximum range of four miles. Some disagreement still exists between British and German sources regarding the extent of the success of the raid.

Today, the four casemates remain and are in reasonably good condition. Casemate No. 1 has been carefully restored and, in 1982, it was opened as a museum. The main firing room and other smaller rooms contain models as well as photographs of the battery and those involved in the episode as well as a range of arms and equipment. In Merville churchyard there is the grave of six British airmen who formed most of the crew of Lancaster bomber W4849 of 156 Squadron. The bomber, piloted by Sergeant Geoffrey Cooper, was shot down on 18 April 1943 to identify the body of the tail gunner, Sergeant Alan Eley from Burton-on-Trent. The bodies of Sergeant Eley and five other members of the crew are buried in one plot. Unfortunately the body of a seventh member of the crew was never recovered and therefore it was impossible to list their names on the headstone. In another part of the churchyard is the unidentified grave of a soldier of the 1914-18 war.

🐃 MONTEBOURG

Montebourg lies thirty kilometres south-east of Cherbourg on the N13 leading to Ste Mère-Église (sixteen kms) and Carentan (twenty-nine kms).

During June 1944, the town lay directly in the path of the American 4th Division and 82nd Airborne Division as they struck north along the Cotentin Peninsula towards Cherbourg. From General von Schlieben's viewpoint, the holding of Montebourg was essential to his plans to defend Cherbourg and deny the Allies the use of a major port. The battle for the town raged for several days and, even with the town reduced to rubble, the German 243rd Division held tenaciously to the ruins. When the US 22nd Infantry Regiment finally took the town on 19 June they found it deserted. Von Schlieben had feared encirclement and withdrawn his forces to defend Cherbourg.

Today, even though 90 per cent of the buildings were destroyed or damaged, the scars of war have long disappeared and a new town has grown from the ashes of the old.

🐃 OMAHA BEACH –
THE AMERICAN MILITARY CEMETERY AND MEMORIAL

The American Military Cemetery and Memorial which overlooks Omaha Beach can be reached by following the D514 from Arromanches-les-Bains and proceeding through the outskirts of Port-en-Bessin and on to Colleville-sur-Mer. Almost immediately after the village turn right – the cemetery is well signposted. Alternatively follow the N13 west from Bayeux and after fifteen kilometres take the right-hand turning to Formigny. Drive for four kilometres along the D517 until you reach the D514 at St Laurent and there turn right towards Colleville-sur-Mer.

On D-Day, the Americans did not have an easy time on Omaha Beach. The choppy seas made the landings difficult and, with the beaches uncleared of mines, without 'funnies' (the specialised tanks used by the British to clear obstacles from the beaches) and with no effective fire support from warships out to sea, the first waves of men of the 16th and 116th Infantry Regiments began to wade ashore at 6.30 a.m. Taken aback by the strength of the German resistance, they found themselves pinned down at the water's edge by murderous enemy fire from strongpoints on the cliffs high above the beach. With bodies floating around them in the sea, some frantically sought cover behind the beach obstacles.

In *Overlord*, Max Hastings describes the situation:

... in an instant, they were compelled to rouse themselves from the cramped, crowded stagnation of the landing craft and stumble forward into a hail of machine-gun and mortar fire from the German defences, which killed and wounded many before they even reached dry ground. Others, still groggy with sea-sickness, their clothes and equipment stiff and matted with salt, desperately sought cover among the beach obstacles or lay paralyzed amid the harvest of wreckage.

Unable to move off the beaches, American casualties rose rapidly and the situation appeared to be getting out of hand. Fortunately, British and United States warships moved in at great speed to bring heavy fire down on the German positions. At the same time, small groups of American soldiers gradually edged their way forward to the top of the escarpment. By the end of the day, the cost of securing a foothold on Omaha was over three thousand dead and wounded.

After the war, the American Battle Monuments Commission developed the land immediately above the scene of their great amphibious landing in June 1944 as a memorial and cemetery for all US servicemen who fell in the Normandy campaign. The next-of-kin of many American servicemen requested the repatriation of their dead and the bodies of some fourteen-thousand men were returned home. The cemetery, built on land donated by the French people, was completed in 1956 and covers seventy-seven thousand hectares. It includes the graves of 9,386 American war dead of whom 307 are unknown. American headstones are white marble crosses and, when the soldier is Jewish, a 'Star of David'. The stones form a geometric pattern and stand out against the beautifully maintained lawns. Among those buried in the cemetery are the sons of former United States President Teddy Roosevelt, Brigadier General Theodore Roosevelt (who died on Utah Beach) and his aviator brother, Quentin Roosevelt, who was killed in the Great War, 1914-18. There are also thirty-two other pairs of brothers and a father and son (Colonel Ollie Reed and his son, Ollie Reed junior).

After leaving the N514, the approach to the cemetery is along an avenue of trees. There is a large car park, and, near the entrance, the superintendent's office with the cemetery registers, visitors' book and information hand-outs. Alongside the path at the entrance is buried a sealed time capsule containing news reports of the 6 June. It was placed there by newsmen in honour of General Eisenhower and is to be opened on 6 June 2044.

The Memorial consists of a semi-circular colonnade with a loggia at each end. In one, battle maps have been engraved into the stone. In the centre, and as a tribute to those young Americans who gave their lives in Normandy, there is a seven-metre-high statue, the 'Spirit of American Youth'. At the base is the inscription, 'Mine eyes have seen the glory of the coming of the Lord'. On the east side of the Memorial is the Garden of the Missing. Semi-circular, it lists the names of the 1,557 American missing. At the side of the central pathway is a chapel with a mosaic ceiling depicting America blessing her sons as they depart by land, sea and air to fight for freedom. Above the altar, France bestows a wreath upon those who gave their lives for liberty and the return of peace is indicated by an angel, a dove and a homeward-bound ship. At the far western end of the cemetery there are two granite figures sculpted by Donald de Lue representing the United States and France. At the edge of the cemetery, where it overlooks Omaha Beach, there is a parapet with an orientation table indicating the various landing beaches. From there it is possible to follow a pathway which leads directly down to the beach. The cemetery and Memorial are maintained by the American Battle Monuments Commission.

To the east of the cemetery there is a road which leads to two other memorials – a plaque to the 5th Engineer Special Brigade and an obelisk surrounded by seats dedicated to the 1st Infantry Division. These are best approached by following a narrow road which leads up from Plage de Colleville-sur-Mer (see Colleville-sur-Mer).

🐾 ORGLANDES

The most direct route to Orglandes is along narrow country roads. First take the D15 from Ste Mère-Église to Cauquigny and there follow the D126 which will eventually bring you to the village.

At Orglandes there is one of the six German war cemeteries in the Normandy region. Managed by the *Volksbund Deutsche Kriegsgräberfürsorge* and opened in September 1961, it extends across an attractive rural setting and contains the graves of over ten thousand German servicemen killed during 1944.

🐾 OUISTREHAM/RIVA BELLA

Ouistreham and its coastal residential area, Riva Bella, lie at the mouth of the River Orne. Apart from being a yachting centre, the town has developed into an important cross-Channel ferry port with Brittany Ferries operating daily sailings to and from Portsmouth.

In 1944, when Rommel visited the town, he is reported to have said, 'If they come, they'll come here'. He was correct. On D-Day, it was the task of Brigadier the Lord Lovat's 1st Special Service Brigade to land at Ouistreham, take the town and then advance inland to join up with the airborne forces holding Pegasus Bridge. With Piper Bill Millin leading the way, Lovat came ashore at 8.20 a.m. Among those who landed with him were Dieppe veteran, then Major now Lieutenant Colonel Mills Roberts commanding No. 6 Commando, and Captain Philippe Kiefer with 1 and 8 Troops of No. 10 Inter-Allied Commando. There was fierce fighting as Kieffer's men took the Casino before the Brigade moved on towards Pegasus Bridge. On their arrival, Piper Millin disregarded German sniper fire to pipe the commandos over the Bridge. By the end of the day, Lovat's men had achieved both their prime objects.

In the vicinity of the Casino and close to the edge of the dunes there are a number of memorials to Commandant Kieffer. On top of the turret of a former German machine-gun emplacement is a flame-shaped memorial dedicated to the French Commando leader. It was inaugurated by President Mitterand on the 6 June 1984. There are two museums in the area, the *Musée du Débarquement 'Sword'* (*Musée No. 4 Commando*), which is on the front and opposite the Casino, and the *Musée du Mur de l'Atlantique* in the *Avenue du 6 Juin*. This museum is on four floors and has been built in a seventeen-metres-high former flak tower from which the Germans once controlled the anti-aircraft defences of the area.

In the centre of the old town is a twelfth century fortress-church which contains two very attractive stained-glass windows. One is dedicated to the British Commandos and the other includes the regimental and corps badges of the units which made up the 51st Highland Division. On the outskirts of the town is the communal cemetery which contains the graves of five British and Commonwealth servicemen. Two are those of RAF fliers who lost their lives in 1942. Sergeant Edward Appleton-Bach, who came from Streatham Common in London, was a spitfire pilot in 131 Squadron. The epitaph on his headstone reads 'What dreams may come when we have shuffled off this mortal coil'. Flight Sergeant John McCallum, a Canadian, flew with 207 Squadron. The remaining three were members of No. 4 Commando who were killed in D-Day. On the roundabout as you leave the town to join the D514 is a *Comité du Débarquement* monument. On the back of it is a memorial plaque '*A La Mémoire des héros du Commando Franco-Anglais No. 4.*'

🐎 PEGASUS BRIDGE –
THE BRIDGES OVER THE CAEN CANAL AND RIVER ORNE

The glider airborne landings close to the bridges over the Caen Canal and River Orne was one of the most spectacular and successful operations on D-Day. The canal bridge, subsequently called Pegasus Bridge, is situated on the outskirts of Bénouville. Barely four kilometres from Ouistreham, to reach the bridge just continue along the D514 towards Sallenelles (be sure to turn off and that you do not proceed on the D515 towards Caen).

On D-Day, the main task allocated to the British 6th Airborne Division was to secure the left flank of the Allied landing area on the far side of the River Orne. If the bridges over the Caen Canal and the river could be taken and held as well as the ridge of high ground beyond, then the invading armies would stand a better chance of breaking out eastwards towards Paris.

At twenty minutes past midnight on the morning of the 6 June, men of the 2nd Battalion the Oxfordshire and Buckinghamshire Light Infantry under the command of Major John Howard landed in Horsa gliders close to the bridge. The leading glider came to rest only four metres from the German blockhouse at the side of the bridge. About four hundred metres further on, a platoon of the same regiment led by Captain Dennis Fox had landed close to the river bridge. Within ten minutes both bridges had been taken. With heavy air raids going on at the same time, poor Helmut Romer, the young German sentry on the canal bridge, thought the first glider was a crashing Allied bomber and, taken by such surprise, he dived for cover without raising the alarm. Even though the Germans recovered and fought back, British casualties were light – just two dead and fourteen wounded. One of the dead was a platoon commander, Lieutenant Den Brotheridge, who fell in the initial attack on the bridge. He is thought to have been the first Allied soldier killed on D-Day. At 12.50 a.m., as the Germans moved to counter-attack, the British 5th Parachute Brigade landed and its 7th Battalion moved to reinforce the defensive positions around the bridges. At about 3 a.m., the Battalion occupied Bénouville and Le Port, the villages closest to the bridges, and held them against repeated and ferocious counter-attacks by the German 21st Panzer Division. By mid-day, the hard-pressed airborne soldiers had been joined by the men of Brigadier Lord Lovat's Commando Brigade which had fought its way inland from the coast. It was 12.02 p.m. when, still under fire, Lord Lovat led his men across Pegasus Bridge. Ahead of them marched Piper Bill Millin playing 'Blue Bonnets over the Border'.

Earlier that morning, Georges Gondrée and his wife, Therese, the proprietors of a café near to the canal bridge, had emerged from their cellar to produce bottles of champagne for the British troops while their home was converted to a medical aid post. Among those involved in the action were Sir Huw Wheldon, who became a well-known broadcaster and director of BBC television, and the actor, Richard Todd. In the film *The Longest Day* Richard Todd played the part of Major John Howard. Dennis Fox, who led the attack on the Orne bridge, later became an executive with ITV.

Today, a bridge still stands across the Caen Canal at Bénouville. It is now called 'Pegasus Bridge', after the famous winged horse of Greek mythology which is the emblem of the Airborne Forces. Virtually a museum in its own right is the Gondree café, which is unchanged and is still run by a member of the family. A popular meeting place for wartime veterans, a plaque above the doorway claims that the house was the first in France to be liberated.

Because Pegasus Bridge was narrow and had to be raised to allow the movement of shipping along the Caen Canal, it has recently been removed and is to be replaced by something more modern. The removal of the old bridge will be regretted by those ex-paratroopers and others who regularly visit the Gondrées café and the area around. At the moment there is some disagreement as to whether the old bridge should be relocated as a museum exhibit close to its present site or be brought to Britain.

Next door is the Pegasus Bridge Museum, which tells the story of the exploits of that night and the following day. It contains a range of models, photographs and examples of the equipment used by paratroopers as well as parts of their gliders and parachutes. On the other side of the bridge is a monument which commemorates the liberation of the banks of the Orne and nearby is the area of rough ground where the first gliders landed. Markers indicate the points where each came down and provide details of their crews.

Further along the road towards Cabourg is the bridge over the River Orne. Rebuilt after the war, it is now known as 'Horsa Bridge' and at its side is a plaque dedicated to the men who took part in the events there.

🪖 POINTE DU HOC

To the west of the main US landing beaches at Omaha is a craggy promontory, the Pointe du Hoc. To reach this area continue westward along the D514 from St Laurent for about fourteen kilometres before a road branches off to the coast. It is well signposted.

Before the war, the Pointe du Hoc was a popular beauty spot but with commanding views both east and west along the coast, the Germans naturally converted it into a strongpoint. Before D-Day, it was recognized that the position would prove particularly dangerous to troops landing on Omaha Beach and that it would have to be put out of action beforehand. The plan was that the navy would saturate the emplacements with shells before an attempt was made to scale the high cliffs. On D-Day, the American battleship *Texas* alone fired six hundred salvoes at the position, with HMS *Talybont* and the US destroyer *Satterlee* making additional contributions. The storming of the position was allocated to three specially trained companies of Lieutenant Colonel James E. Rudder's 2nd Ranger Battalion. Unfortunately things did not go according to plan. The Americans mistook the Pointe de la Percee (three kilometres to the east) for the Pointe du Hoc and arrived late. Once they had landed, they used rocket-fired ropes with grappling irons to try to climb to the summit. The German defenders who had survived the bombardment had every advantage and were able to drop grenades and fire directly on the Americans beneath. Eventually the American Rangers made it to the top, and after further hand-to-hand fighting, stormed forward to take the gun positions. There were supposed to have been six 155 mm guns but they found none. They had moved one kilometre inland the day before! During the rest of the day, the Germans launched counter-attacks against the American bridgehead while an attempt to reach them by US infantry from Omaha Beach failed. In spite of everything, the Rangers managed to hold on until they were finally relieved at mid-day on 8 June. In all, the Rangers suffered 135 casualties – well over half the attacking force.

The former battle area, some twelve hectares, is now preserved. There is a car park at the approach and maintained paths through the area which still remains scarred with craters and shattered bunkers. It is possible to go right to the edge of the cliffs where, on top of a German casemate, there is a granite monument which commemorates the events of 6-7 June. Inside there is a series of plaques listing the names of the Rangers who lost their lives in the action. On 6 June 1979, in a ceremony attended by General Omar Bradley, the area passed into the care of the American Battle Monuments Commission. Interestingly, as late as 1961 and prior to the making of the film *The Longest Day*, flame-throwers had to be used to make the place safe by exploding any remaining mines and ammunition.

🐾 PORT-EN-BESSIN

A lively fishing port of some charm, Port-en-Bessin lies nine kilometres north of Bayeux on the D6 and eleven kilometres to the west of Arromanches-les-Bains on the D514 coast road leading towards Omaha Beach.

The harbour is encircled to both east and west by high cliffs and, prior to D-Day, the Germans turned these into formidable defensive positions, as noted by Lieutenant Commander Nigel Clogstoun-Willmott on a reconnaissance mission in a midget submarine, prior to D-Day:

> It was rather interesting seeing Port-en-Bessin and the cliffs each side of it quite clearly in daylight. We dived a couple of miles after that started creeping in and looking at the defences through this tiny periscope, which was about as thick as a man's thumb. We went in quite close, I should think as close as 100 yards from the edge of the water, and we could see people on shore bulldozing and improving the defences, making ditches.

(The full interview appears in *Nothing Less Than Victory: The Oral History of D-Day* by Russell Miller.)

On 6 June the town lay on the western limit of Gold Beach but was outside the designated landing area of the British 50th Division. It was not until the following day that men of 47 (RM) Commando moved against the German emplacements. The Royal Marine Commandos had already experienced a difficult time. On the previous day, many of their landing craft had been sunk as they came in to land at Le Hamel and the survivors had been forced to swim ashore. As a result they lost forty-six men and almost every wireless the unit possessed. At Port-en-Bessin, their attempt to take the German positions was supported by a naval bombardment from HMS *Emerald* and strikes by rocket-firing RAF Typhoons. Two of the strongpoints were taken but the Commandos were unable to consolidate their position and, in the face of determined German counter-attacks, fighting continued into the evening. The

German commander, together with three hundred of his men, finally surrendered at 4 a.m. the following morning. Soon afterwards 47 Commando made contact with patrols of the US 1st Infantry Division advancing from Omaha Beach. By 12 June, Port-en-Bessin was operational and able to take supplies intended for both the British 50th Infantry Division and the American 1st Division. It was to become an important British petrol storage depot.

Today Port-en-Bessin is popular with both holiday makers and weekend visitors. The harbour is enclosed by two semi-circular jetties and on the one to the east there is a *Comité du Débarquement* Monument. At the bottom of the cliffs there is a German bunker with a memorial plaque to 47 Commando set against the wall. High above and beyond the Vauban Tower there are the remains of the original German defences – it is quite a climb!

🐾 RANVILLE

Ranville lies some five kilometres to the south-east of Pegasus Bridge. After crossing the bridge over the River Orne, take the second turning on the right off the D514 and follow the signposts to the village.

This was the main dropping area of the 6th Airborne Division on D-Day. The Division comprised the 3rd and 5th Parachute Brigades and the glider-borne troops the 6th Air Landing Brigade. While the men of the 3rd Parachute Brigade were attacking the battery at Merville and destroying the bridges over the River Dives at Troarn, Bures and Robehomme, the 5th Brigade were taking the bridges over the Caen Canal and the River Orne and preparing the area around Ranville for the arrival of a large force of gliders. They first had to clear the village and then secure the landing area. This meant clearing away 'Rommel's asparagus' – a large number of spaced poles intended to hinder airborne landings – and then acting as 'Pathfinders' by marking the landing area with flares. The armada of Horsa gliders towed by RAF Halifax, Lancaster and Sterling aircraft began to land at 3.30 a.m. They brought with them their commanding officer, Major General Richard Gale – the first Allied general to set foot on liberated French soil – as well as anti-tank guns and jeeps. Major General Gale's glider was piloted by S. C. 'Billy' Griffith, the late Sussex and England wicket-keeper. As this was happening, Dakotas were busy dropping paratroop reinforcements. By morning, the area was a mass of men milling around whole and broken gliders.

The grass square close to the church is today called *Place Général Sir Richard Gale* and in the town, on a wall in the *Place du 6 Juin 1944*, is a plaque which commemorates the fact that Ranville was the first French village to be liberated at 2.30 a.m. on the 6 June by the 13th (Lancashire) Battalion, the Parachute Regiment. The church contains a stained-glass window dedicated to the 6th Airborne Division.

RANVILLE WAR CEMETERY

Ranville War Cemetery, which is closely associated with the 6th Airborne Division, lies next to the church in the *Rue des Airbornes* which skirts the edge of *Place Général Sir Richard Gale* and is close to the centre of the village. The cemetery contains 2,562 burials including 2,151 British, 322 German and 76 Canadian. Nearly all died on 6/7 June 1944. Among those buried there are the brother Lieutenants Maurice and Philippe Rousseau from Montreal, Canada. Maurice, the elder brother, arrived in Britain in 1941 and ten months before D-Day, married a girl from Preston. Philippe landed in France with the 1st Canadian Parachute Battalion on the 6 June and was killed the following day. Squadron Leader J. R. Collins, DFC and Bar, who lost his life on 11 August, was the pilot of a Typhoon. Shot down over Ranville, he was killed when his parachute failed to open. The Glasgow army padre, Robert Cape, was attached to the Black Watch and was killed on 25 June while a sixteen-year-old Portsmouth lad, Private Robert Johns, lost his life on the 23 July while serving with the Parachute Regiment. Kurt Meyer, a young Jewish soldier of German extraction, was a lance corporal with No. 10 Inter-Allied Commando. For obvious reasons, he served under an assumed name, Peter Moody, and was killed on 13 June. Private Emile Corteil was responsible for the paratroop dog, Glen, and they were inseparable. The Alsatian, usually keen to jump from aircraft, seemed hesitant on D-Day but they made it safely to the ground. Sadly the young paratrooper and his dog were among those mistakenly killed when strafed by Allied aircraft. When they were found, Glen was still linked to his master by his lead. They were buried together. In the adjoining churchyard, a further forty-seven British soldiers are buried close to the perimeter wall. They include Lieutenant Den Brotheridge, the first man to fall on D-Day during the initial attack on Pegasus Bridge.

🐾 REVIERS

Reviers lies midway between Ouistreham and Bayeux and four kilometres to the south of Courseulles-sur-Mer. Travelling west from Ouistreham, follow the D35 through Colleville-Montgomery and Douvres-la-Délivrande and the village is just beyond the Bény-sur-Mer Canadian War Cemetery, which is on the right-hand side of the road. From Bayeux, drive directly along the D12 and D176 to reach Reviers, which is twenty-two kilometres away.

The village was liberated by the Canadians on D-Day.

On a grass verge close to the centre of the village is a memorial '*To the memory of the soldiers of the Regina Rifle Regiment who freed Reviers D-Day 1944*'.

🔫 RYES

The village of Ryes, which is twinned with the Hampshire villages of Michelmersh and Timsbury, lies some ten kilometres to the north-east of Bayeux. It can be reached by taking the D12 to Sommervieu and then following the D112 for little more than a kilometre before turning on to the D205 which leads to the village. Alternatively, it is five kilometres inland from Arromanches on the D87.

The village was liberated by the 1st Battalion of the Dorset Regiment on the evening of D-Day.

RYES WAR CEMETERY

Ryes War Cemetery is actually on the outskirts of Bazenville which lies some two kilometres to the south-east of Ryes. From Ryes, follow the D87 towards Bazenville and, just past the crossroads with the D112, the cemetery will be found a few hundred metres along on the left-hand side of the road.

There are 979 graves in the cemetery made up of 630 British, 326 German, 21 Canadians as well as an Australian and a Pole. Many of the burials are of men killed on or soon after D-Day. They include those of the crew of an RAF Dakota which crashed near Ryes on 5 August 1944. The grave of the pilot, Flying Officer P. C. Hankansson, lies close to those of the remainder of his crew. Nearby are also to be found the graves of many of the crew of HMS *Glen Avon* as well as those of a number of merchant seamen who died while serving on the SS *Empire Rosebery*. HMS *Glen Avon* was a paddle minesweeper which had earlier helped rescue 890 soldiers during two journeys to the Dunkirk beaches in 1940. On 2 September, she was caught in a gale off Arromanches and, unable to weigh anchor or slip her cable, she floundered and sank with the loss of fifteen lives. The SS *Empire Rosebery* struck a mine off Arromanches on 24 August and sank with the loss of ten of her crew and three gunners.

🔫 ST AUBIN-SUR-MER

Between Courseulles-sur-Mer and Langrune-sur-Mer is St Aubin-sur-Mer – one of the string of coastal resorts along the Côte de Nacre. Following the D514, it is fifteen kilometres from Ouistreham. Approached from the south and west, it is twenty-one kilometres from Caen (D7) and twenty-nine from Bayeux (D516 and D514).

On D-Day, the town was on the eastern edge of Juno Beach. The beach here was a broad expanse of sand, heavily mined and with a wall to the rear. It gave every advantage to the defenders. After an initial bombardment, 48 Royal Marine Commando led the way ashore at 7.30 a.m. and were followed by the amphibious tanks of the 10th Canadian Armoured Regiment – the Fort Garry Horse – and the North Shore Regiment of Canada. The liberation of the town was achieved after three hours' heavy fighting.

Today, an intact German bunker with its gun still in position remains prominently placed on the sea-front. To the left is a monument to the Canadian North Shore Regiment and to 48 Royal Marine Commando. Next to it, a plaque records that on 4 August 1940, Maurice Duclos, a French secret agent code-named *Saint Jacques*, landed here. Further to the east, close to the offices of the *Syndicat d'Initiative*, is another memorial which records that 'on these beaches at H Hour 6th June 1944 landed the amphibious tanks of the 10th Canadian Armoured Regiment (Fort Garry Horse)'.

🐎 ST CÔME-DE-FRESNÉ

Saint Côme-de-Fresné lies on the D514 just to the east of Arromanches-les-Bains.

On the morning of D-Day, the village and neighbouring Le Hamel were on the western flank of the landing area which lay within the limits of Gold Beach. 47 Royal Marine Commando landed here before moving inland to by-pass Arromanches on their way to Port-en-Bessin, where they hoped to link up with the Americans advancing from Omaha. Their speed was such that 'by 0800 hours in the hamlet behind the beaches of St Côme-de-Fresné , the citizens were able to celebrate their liberation ... Across the din of gunfire, the pealing bells of St Côme signalled the liberation of the eastern beachhead.'
At the top of the hill between Arromanches-les-Bains and St Côme-de-Fresné is a column surmounted by a white statue of the Virgin Mary and, nearby, there is an observation platform which allows spectacular views westward; across the town of Arromanches, and eastward, along what was Gold Beach. At the edge of the cliffs are the remains of numerous German bunkers.

🐎 ST LAURENT-SUR-MER

St Laurent-sur-Mer lies on the D514 midway between Colleville-sur-Mer and Vierville-sur-Mer and immediately behind Omaha Beach. It is just to the west of the road leading to the American Military Cemetery and Memorial.

At the crossroads (D517/D514) follow the road to the coast at Plage de St Laurent-sur-Mer. This area, together with the beaches immediately to the east and west, formed Utah Beach (see Utah Beach: the American Cemetery and Memorial).

Part-way down the hill, turn left and then take a right-hand fork to reach the elegant memorial to the United States 8th Engineer Special Brigade. Return to the road leading to the beach and, at the bottom of the hill, turn right and drive to a car park close to an old German bunker. At the top of a flight of steps and in front of the bunker are memorials to the US Army's Second Infantry Division and the Provisional Engineer Special Brigade Group. From here it is possible to look eastwards towards the flat plateau which is today surmounted by the American Military Cemetery. Return along the road and, at the crossroads, continue straight ahead. On the left-hand side of the road you will soon reach the marker of the original site of the first American Second World War cemetery in France. The road ahead leads to Plage de Vierville-sur-Mer.

✈ STE MARIE DU MONT

The village of Sainte Marie du Mont lies five kilometres behind Utah Beach and can be reached by following the D913. If approaching from Ste Mère-Église, take the N13 southward to Les Forges and then turn left along the D70.

On D-Day, the village lay just within the area covered by the landings made by the US 101st Airborne Division commanded by Major General Maxwell Taylor. It was of considerable strategic importance since it lay immediately to the rear of one of the few remaining causeways across the flooded area behind the dunes of Utah Beach. The village was garrisoned by German troops and many homes had soldiers billeted on them. The arrival of American paratroopers turned the village into a battle area and there was skirmishing in the streets around the square. The church, which contained a German observation post, changed hands several times. During the morning, when the paratroopers were joined by other American units which had advanced inland from the coast, the last German resistance was overcome.

Today, the village remains very much the same as it was on 6 June 1944. Of particular interest to visitors are the fourteen notices dotted about on walls which give precise details of exactly what happened there during the struggle to liberate the village. Close to the church and bedecked with flags, *La Boutique Du Holdy* offers for sale a range of postcards, books and battlefield memorabilia.

Just outside the village, a short distance along the D424E leading to Brucheville, there is a memorial to those who lost their lives flying with the 36th Fighter Group of the Ninth US Air Force. During August 1944, they flew from a nearby airstrip and the monument was placed there on the 4 April 1990.

✈ STE MÈRE-ÉGLISE

Just off the N13 and midway between Carentan and Montebourg is the town of Sainte Mère-Église. If travelling from Utah Beach, it can be approached on the D15 by way of Ravenoville.

It was at 1.30 a.m. on the morning of D-Day that the first American paratroopers of the US 82nd and 101st Airborne Divisions began to drop in and around the small town. The aim of the men of the 82nd Division, commanded by Major General Matthew Ridgway, was to take the town, hold the bridges and locks over the Rivers Douve and Merderet and cut road and rail communications between Carentan and Cherbourg. The 101st Division, under Major General Maxwell Taylor, was to secure the high ground and remaining road exits across the flooded area behind Utah Beach. Unfortunately things did not go according to plan. Many men landed far from their designated dropping areas and some in the areas flooded by the Germans. The region is low-lying and the Rivers Douve and Merderet were already high and much of the ground either flooded or waterlogged. In addition, the Germans opened the sluice gates immediately behind Utah Beach to further flood the area and hinder the American advance inland towards Ste Mère-Église. Many US paratroopers and gliderborne soldiers perished in the waters but this did not prevent the Americans from moving away from the beaches and linking up with those who had made the airborne drop further inland. The men themselves provided easy targets as they descended in the night sky and a number of gliders disintegrated on landing. As they tried to regroup in the darkness, so skirmishes began between lost American soldiers and German patrols. The paratroopers used clicking metal crickets to help identification but the Germans discovered their secret and this added to the nightmare confusion. Losses were very heavy. The 82nd Division, with four thousand men missing, was reduced to one-third of its strength, while 101st Division had lost 60 per cent of its equipment and could only muster a thousand men. Even so, the 505th Parachute Infantry Regiment which landed in the square at Ste Mère-Église was able to raise the American flag outside the town hall by 6 a.m. in the morning.

The day produced its heroes. Private John Steele, caught by his parachute harness on a corner of the church tower, feigned death as his comrades fought in the square below. Elsewhere, Corporal Schuyler Jackson pushed his wounded colonel around in a wheelbarrow. The town's priest, Abbé Roulland, rang the church bells to summon help as fires caused by Allied bombing started to engulf homes. Alexandre Renaud, the mayor, local chemist and veteran of the 1914-18 war, organised people into a chain to pass buckets of water, hand-to-hand, from the only pump available. Maurice Duboscq, a railway crossing attendant and better known as 'Papa Maurice', used his small boat to rescue paratroopers struggling in the flooded fields and turned his home into a sanctuary for American wounded. Tragically, a year later his son, Claude, was killed by an unexploded land mine.

Today, much of the town of Ste Mère-Église remains dedicated to the events of the 6 June 1944. In the square, the tower of the parish church still carries a model of the fortunate paratrooper, John Steele, who was a regular visitor to the town until his death in 1969. Inside the church are two stained-glass windows – one, designed by Paul Renaud and offered by the 82nd Airborne Division, is mainly blue and shows the Virgin

Mary surrounded by descending paratroopers; the other was presented by members of the 82nd Airborne Division Association on the twenty-fifth anniversary of the landing and depicts Saint Michael, the patron saint of the local diocese, and is inscribed *'Ils sont revenus'* ('They have come back').

On the edge of the square lies the impressive Airborne Museum which is housed in two buildings, each under a parachute-shaped dome. The Museum covers every aspect of the airborne landings and includes many original documents, maps and a great deal of memorabilia. There are also displays of uniforms and weapons as well as a restored original Waco CG-4A Hadrian glider and a Dakota aircraft. Around the square there is a monument to 6 June and another to the memory of Alexandre Renaud, *'maire de la libération, premier historien du débarquement'.*

In the seldom visited communal cemetery close to the museum are the graves of Abbé Roulland and *'Papa Maurice et Petit Claude'*. In front of the old town hall is KO – the first of the rounded, stone monuments which mark the *'Voie de la Liberté'*. The chain of markers trace the advance of the Americans across France and end at Bastogne in Belgium, the town which became famous during the 'Battle of the Bulge' in December 1944. Behind the monument is a memorial to local residents who gave their lives during the war.

The American soldiers who died on D-Day and during the following days were first buried in mass graves in the locality. During 1948, their bodies were removed and the original sites are now marked by memorials. The marker for US Cemetery No.1, which once contained three thousand men, is a short distance from the square, just behind the fire station. The marker for the five thousand men once buried in US Cemetery No.2 can be found just outside the town on the road leading to Chef-du-Pont. There is a third marker on the roadside (D70) leading to Les Forges which indicates a former cemetery which once contained the graves of six thousand American servicemen (see Chef-du-Pont).

In 1961, memories of local people were revived when the town was used as the location in the making of part of Darryl Zanuck's epic film, *The Longest Day*.

🦅 SALLENELLES

After crossing Pegasus Bridge to the east bank of the River Orne, the first village to be reached on the D514 is Sallenelles. It lies eight kilometres from Ouistreham and is on the road leading to Merville-Franceville.

This is in the area where the British 3rd Parachute Brigade landed on D-Day.

On the left-hand side of the road as you reach the end of the village, there is a plaque set on to the gate of a house in memory of twenty-year-old Edouard Gerard of the Brigade Piron. From Dinant in Belgium, he was the first soldier from his country to be killed during the Normandy campaign.

There are also two memorials – one to soldiers from Belgium and Luxembourg who, under Colonel Jean Piron, served in the 1st Belgian Brigade; the other honours the men of the 4th Special Service Brigade who lost their lives while serving in the area.

🔫 SECQUEVILLE-EN-BESSIN

Secqueville-en-Bessin is a village some twelve kilometres north-west of Caen and three kilometres from Bretteville-l'Orgueilleuse, a village just off the main Caen to Bayeux road (N13). In Bretteville-l'Orgueilleuse take the D93 northwards to the village which is two kilometres ahead.

SECQUEVILLE-EN-BESSIN WAR CEMETERY

The War Cemetery is situated to the east of the village. To reach it, turn right in the village and after a few hundred metres there is a track to the left signposted Farringdon Way. The cemetery can be seen in open fields on the left-hand side. It contains 117 graves and of these ninety-eight are British, eighteen German and one unknown. The graves are of men killed in the advance towards Caen early in July 1944.

🔫 THAON

Thaon lies twenty-one kilometres north-west of Caen. The village can be reached by first taking the D22 to Cairon. Just beyond the village turn right along the D170 and proceed to Thaon, which is two kilometres ahead.

The village was liberated on 6 June by the 10th Armoured Regiment (Fort Garry Horse) in support of the 8th Canadian Infantry Brigade.

In the centre of the square is a small memorial which commemorates the liberation of the village by the Canadians on D-Day.

🔫 TIERCEVILLE

Fourteen kilometres to the east of Bayeux along the D12 is the village of Tierceville.

After 6 June, the area around the village became a Royal Engineers base-depot and it was from here that the materials required for road and bridge repair and landing-field construction were stockpiled. At a road junction on the D176 to the east of the village is an unusual monument which in August 1944, when it was first constructed, may have reminded Londoners of home and, in particular, Piccadilly Circus.

The 179 Special Field Company of the Royal Engineers made a copy of a statue of Eros out of cement. More elaborate than the West End original, it was later damaged by frost. Restored in 1971, it now stands on a white column in the centre of a circular embankment enclosed by railings.

🐗 TILLY-SUR-SEULLES

From Bayeux, take the D6 south-eastwards and Tilly-sur-Seulles is twelve kilometres ahead. From Caen, follow the D9 due west for twenty kilometres to Fontenay-le-Pesnel and there turn on to the D13 to reach the town some four kilometres ahead.

On the morning of the 7 June 1944, the British 50th Division occupied Bayeux and then pushed on south towards Tilly-sur-Seulles. The town lay to the west of Caen in an area defended by Kurt Meyer's 12th SS Panzer Division (the Hitler Jugend) and Fritz Bayerlein's crack Panzer Lehr Division. Already reduced to ruins, the Germans used Panzer Lehr in a determined effort to hold on to Tilly and the town became the scene of the most bitter fighting of the campaign. It was said 'the lyrical name of Tilly-sur-Seulles became a synonym for fear and endless death'. The town was not liberated until 18 June and fighting continued nearby until mid-July.

The town has an unusual war museum. The *Musée de la Bataille de Tilly-sur-Seulles* is located in an old twelfth-century church, the *Chapelle Notre Dame du Val*. Modernised, it was opened by the *Comité du Débarquement* in June 1979. The exhibition traces the history of the town from June 1940 until its liberation on the 18 June. Outside there is a statue of Jeanne d'Arc which was damaged by a British shell during the fighting.

TILLY-SUR-SEULLES WAR CEMETERY

To reach the Tilly-sur-Seulles War Cemetery, take the D9 westwards out of the town and it is one kilometre ahead on the left-hand side. The cemetery contains 1,222 burials including 986 British and 232 German. They were all killed during the heavy fighting in the area during the period up to 18 June. The cemetery includes many graves of men of the 2nd Devonshires who were killed on 11 June near La Belle Epine when they came under attack from German tanks and infantry. Among the graves of men of the King's Own Yorkshire Light Infantry killed on 25 June is that of Major Gerald Roberts. Aged twenty-five and from Scarborough, he was one of three brothers who lost their lives during the war. Private John Gethin from Thurnscoe in Yorkshire was only eighteen when he lost his life n 27 August while serving with the Gordon Highlanders.

BRITISH ATTACK IN CALVADOS

ADVANCE BEYOND TILLY

FOREST WARFARE

From Our Special Correspondent
CHERBOURG FRONT, JUNE 25

Before first light of this glorious Sunday morning British formations on the Calvados front began an advance against limited objectives east of Tilly-sur-Seulles. Since the definite capture of Tilly a few days ago there has been little movement in this sector apart from constant patrol clashes in the woods and sunken lanes.

Even for the smallest attack the pattern is the same. At 3 a.m. a heavy artillery

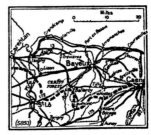

barrage of guns—field, mediums, and heavies—was put down on the enemy astride the River Seulles, in an area 1,000 yards deep. It is a French military maxim that forest warfare is a voracious *mangeur d'hommes*, and indeed this savage bombardment must have brought the trees down about the enemy's ears. It lasted for 45 minutes, and then our infantry began to creep forward through a thick ground mist.

With dawn came the fighter-bombers to add their weight of destruction on German positions. The whole plan was concerted with such care and power that Panzer units that have been in the line ever since the landings and have been mercilessly whittled down could do little to prevent us from advancing.

The fighting continues, and for an hour or more from its opening, allied heavy bombers in large formations droned over the enemy's forward positions to attack the vital communications behind them.

1,000 YARD ADVANCE

WITH THE BRITISH FORCES, June 25.— British infantry, after less than four hours' fighting through close wooded country, this morning advanced over 1,000 yards south-east of Tilly. The advance, in which no armour was committed by either side, began shortly before 4 a.m. The battle is said to be going on " very satisfactorily," and though German tanks are known to be in the vicinity they have not yet shown up. The drive has taken British troops to an important point south of Tilly.—
Reuter

From *The Times* of 26 June 1944.

🐾 TOUFFREVILLE

Touffreville is seven kilometres to the east of Caen. The village lies just off the N175, barely a kilometre to the north of Sannerville and can also be reached from Ranville by following the D37 to Hérouvillette and then turning on to the D227.

The only memorial in the village is to one British paratrooper – Private Arthur Platt. The body of the former member of the 8th Parachute Battalion, now buried in Ranville War Cemetery, was originally found with that of a fallen comrade on 10 June 1944. Years after the war, his son researched the background to his father's death and discovered that he had been shot by the SS when held as a prisoner-of-war. In 1988, the people of Touffreville erected a memorial to Private Platt at the spot where the soldier's body was found. The monument is not easily located. In Touffreville, turn right at the second turning after the church before taking a left-hand fork along a track. The memorial is about three hundred metres along the track.

In Touffreville churchyard is the grave of one British paratrooper, Lance Corporal Edward O'Sullivan, who came from Bedford and was killed on D-Day.

🐾 TROARN

Troarn lies due east of Caen. It can be most easily reached by taking the A13/E46 autoroute out of the city and, after thirteen kilometres, turning off at exit 30. It can also be approached from Ouistreham by first crossing Pegasus Bridge and, after Ranville, going cross-country on the D37 directly to the town.

One of the most important tasks allocated to the British 6th Airborne Division was to destroy the numerous bridges over the River Dives and so protect the eastern flank of the Allied bridgehead from a possible German counter-attack. The most important bridge was to the east of Troarn. They were to be blown up by a Parachute Squadron of the Royal Engineers supported by troops from both the 1st Canadian and 8th Parachute Battalions. The destruction of the bridge at Troarn is described by Sir Huw Wheldon in *Red Berets into Normandy*:

Major Roseveare, another officer, and seven sappers had landed in the early hours ... and set off on foot, with as much explosives as they could collect and carry, for Troarn, some eight kilometres away.

As time was running out Roseveare commandeered a jeep and trailer, stuffed them with explosives and, with nine of them aboard (one on the trailer as a rear gunner) and the windscreen down, set off at top speed on the road to Troarn. The town was fully occupied by the Germans and they were soon in trouble at a road block, but extricated themselves. Then, charging down the main street of the town with the Sten guns of his men blazing and amid a hail of German machine-gun fire and Germans jumping out of his way in the darkness, Roseveare reached the bridge. The engineers laid their explosives, the trailer was unhooked in the middle of the bridge, a minimum fuse was lit, and in seconds the solid stone mainroad bridge had an eight-metre gap and Roseveare and the survivors of his party were disappearing down a lane by the river.

In the town square there is a plaque on the wall of the *syndicat d'initiaitve* dedicated to the officers and men of the 3rd Parachute Squadron Royal Engineers *'qui, sur des renseignements obtenus de la Résistance, ont détruit les ponts de la Dives pour protéger le flanc gauche du Débarquement a l'aube du 6 Juin 1944'*. In the town's communal cemetery are the graves of three British soldiers. All in their twenties, Private Henry Carter and Sergeants John Davies and John Iliffe served with the 8th Battalion, Parachute Regiment and died on 6 June. Just outside the town, at the side of the bridge which they once destroyed, is a memorial to Major J. C. A. Roseveare and his men.

🪂 UTAH BEACH

Utah Beach lies between Les Dunes de Varreville and La Madeline and runs alongside the coast road, the D421. The area can be reached from the south by following the N13 from Carentan and then, after some four kilometres, taking the right-hand turn just before St Côme-du-Mont and travelling along the D913 through Vierville and Ste Marie du Mont to reach La Madeline. From the north, it is best to leave the N13 at Ste Mère-Église, pass through the town and then travel along the D15 to Ravenoville before following the narrow road towards the coast to reach Les Dunes de Varreville. All routes to Utah Beach are well signposted.

This was the landing are allocated to the American 4th Division on D-Day. The stretch of beach lay between Les Dunes de Varreville and La Madeline at the south-eastern end of the Cotentin Peninsula to the north of the Baie des Veys, the broad estuary formed by the Rivers Douve and Vire. The beaches were themselves protected by mines and other obstacles and immediately behind them was a string of bunkers and strongpoints. At the rear were numerous powerful batteries with their guns ranged on the beaches.

Supported by heavy bombing and a naval bombardment, the first landing craft made their way through choppy seas and under cover of a smoke-screen towards the shore. It was 6.30 a.m. when the initial waves of General J. Lawton Collins's 7th US Corps went ashore. They landed not opposite St Martin-de-Varreville as planned but, because of a navigational error, some two kilometres further south. In spite of the error, Brigadier General Theodore Roosevelt, the fifty-seven-year-old son of former

US President 'Teddy' Roosevelt, who had gone ashore with the first assault troops, decided to press ahead with the landing. It proved a wise decision since the area was less strongly defended than the correct landing zone and it placed the men beyond the range of the German heavy batteries to the north. The initial crisis over, the landings were well co-ordinated and ran smoothly. A feature of the German defences was the use of miniature radio-operated tanks filled with explosives. Nicknamed 'Goliaths', they had already been used on the Eastern Front but now, with their radio controls jammed, they proved useless.

Once ashore and with the beaches cleared, their first objectives were to advance inland and join the 82nd and 101st US Airborne Divisions and cut the main road from Carentan to the north. Later, it was intended that they would link up with the American forces then landing at Omaha Beach further to the south. Although engineers quickly removed beach obstacles and blew holes in the sea-wall, the troops still had to cross flooded lowland meadows behind the dunes before they could deploy inland. Although German resistance stiffened, during the course of the day the Americans established a firm bridgehead for men, vehicles and supplies to pour ashore. They also began to make their way inland across a secure raised causeway and advanced eight kilometres to be able to assist the hard-pressed 101st at Ste Mère-Église. Because the initial enemy resistance was light, the total casualties of the 4th Infantry Division were 197 with only twelve dead. It was sad that six days later the good-natured and much admired Theodore Roosevelt died of a heart attack.

Today, a great deal remains to remind visitors of the events at Utah Beach on 6 June 1944. On the beach at Saint Martin-de-Varreville is a monument to the French 2nd Armoured Division which landed there under General Philippe Leclerc. Previously the general had fought with the British 8th Army in North Africa and his Armoured Division was later to take part in a spectacular drive to liberate Paris. Further south is the section of the Beach where the US forces actually landed. Close to Les Dunes de Madeleine there are monuments to the 1st Engineer Special Brigade, the 90th US Infantry Division and the 4th US Infantry Division. Very impressive is the tall monument 'erected by the United States of America in humble tribute to its sons who lost their lives in the liberation of these beaches'. Here, built on the site of a former German strongpoint, is a museum which houses an impressive collection of maps, photographs, souvenirs and working models. It also has a theatre which shows documentary films. Outside is a collection of vehicles including a landing craft, Sherman tank and several field guns. An interesting feature of the area is that sections of the road leading from the Leclerc Memorial towards the American memorials on Utah Beach and from the Beach towards Ste Marie du Mont are named after US servicemen who died during the landings there.

🐾 VALOGNES

Valognes, a market town whose grand houses once caused it to be known as 'the Versailles of Normandy', lies on the N13, the main Cherbourg to Caen road. It is twenty-one kilometres to the south-east of the port and just seven kilometres to the north of Montebourg.

During the hectic days of June 1944, General von Schlieben had his headquarters in the town. After the fall of Montebourg on 19 June, the town fell to the Americans without much of a fight. Nevertheless, by that time the damage had been done and much of Valognes was in ruins. Sadly, few of its old and historic houses survived.

Today, Valognes is a colourful, modern town and, although some of the old buildings have been restored and there is still much of interest to be seen, the glories of its former years have largely vanished.

🐾 VER-SUR-MER

Some thirteen kilometres to the east of Arromanches-les-Bains on the D514 is Ver-sur-Mer. Travelling from Ouistreham, the coastal village is twenty-three kilometres to the west on the same road.

The village lies just inland from the beaches of La Rivière and on D-Day the area was on the eastern edge of Gold Beach. This was the area assigned to the British 50th Division and the first ashore at 7.25 a.m. were the 5th East Yorkshire Regiment and 6th Green Howards. Here the coast rises gently from the beach but there is little cover. Once the mines were removed by flail-tanks, the invaders moved off the beaches towards the German strongpoint at Mont Fleury. It was here that CSM Stan Hollis of the Green Howards earned his Victoria Cross – the only man to do so on 6 June. Ver-sur-Mer was badly damaged during the preliminary bombardment but, even so, 'a little cluster of French civilians emerged from the ruins to cheer and throw flowers'.

Close to the centre of the village there are two memorials. One is dedicated to the British troops who liberated Ver-sur-Mer on the 6 June and, in particular, the 2nd Hertfordshire Regiment. The other, an upright anchor mounted on a stone base and marked *Hommage et reconnaissance à nos libérateurs*, was donated by Julien Costy, a local fisherman. On the opposite side of the road is the large house which, after D-Day, served as the headquarters of Admiral Sir Bertram Ramsay, the Allied Naval Commander-in-Chief.

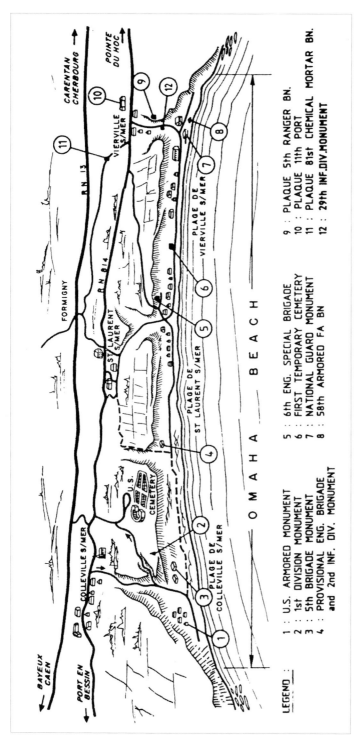

The location of the American Monuments in the vicinity of Omaha Beach. Monument 1 is in Plage de Colleville-sur-Mer and 2 and 3 can be reached by following a road from the coast to a parking area just below and to the east of the American Cemetery (the road is one-way). They can also be reached on foot from the Cemetery. Monuments 4 and 5 are at each end of the Plage de St Laurent-sur-Mer and can be visited by driving the length of the beach while Monument 6 is situated high above the beach but can be reached by car. Monuments 7, 8, 9 and 12 are all located reasonably close together in Plage de Vierville-sur-Mer while 10 and 11 are back on the main road just off the D514.

🦅 VIERVILLE-SUR-MER

A short drive along the coast from St Laurent-sur-Mer is Vierville-sur-Mer. On a visit to the Omaha Beach area, it is easiest to continue directly along the coastal road from Plage de St Laurent-sur-Mer to Plage de Vierville-sur-Mer. Inland, it is off the D514, three kilometres to the west of St Laurent-sur-Mer.

On D-Day, the beach at Vierville-sur-Mer was towards the western end of Omaha Beach. As elsewhere along this stretch of coast, many of the men who came ashore here were cut down before they were out of the water (*see Omaha Beach: The American Cemetery and Memorial*).

Much remains to remind visitors of the events of 6 June 1944. On the sea-front there is a *Comité du Débarquement* monument and nearby, close to the remains of a German bunker, a section of a Mulberry Harbour has been used to support the landing section of a narrow pier. Raised on a platform there is a monument to the National Guard which records that 'thousands of citizen-soldiers of the National Guard stormed ashore on these beaches on 6 June 1944 as part of the army of the United States. They fought valiantly and with great distinction in all the ensuing battles of World War II.'

As you leave the beach and follow the road back towards the D514, there is a central grassed area with a monument to the 29th United States Infantry Division. It was erected in 1988 by the 29th Division Association. A little further along on the right-hand side is a plaque to the 5th Ranger Battalion, which 'advanced against strongly defended enemy fortifications manned by General Rommel's toughest troops. The Ranger breakthrough opened the beach allowing troops of the 29th Infantry Division to pour through and thus paved the way for the liberation of France'. Back on the main road (D514), turn right and immediately on the left-hand side is the Château de Vierville, which was the headquarters of the Eleventh Port regiment of the United States Army from the 8 June until the 21 July.

INDEX